*Tackling Numeracy Issues*
Book 5

**Improving the plenary session in Key Stage 1, Years 1 and 2**

*Caroline Clissold*

*Tackling Numeracy Issues*

# Book 5

# Improving the plenary session in Key Stage 1, Years 1 and 2

*Caroline Clissold*

The *Questions* Publishing Company Limited
Birmingham
2002

The Questions Publishing Company Ltd
Leonard House, 321 Bradford Street, Digbeth, Birmingham B5 6ET

First published in 2002

ISBN: 1-84190-053-2

Design and incidental illustration by Ivan Morison and Al Stewart
Cover by Martin Cater

Printed in the UK

**Also available from the Questions Publishing Company Limited:**

Book 1 *Fractions and Decimals, Key Stage 1*
ISBN: 1-84190-079-6

Book 2 *Fractions, Decimals and Percentages, Key Stage 2*
ISBN: 1-84190-047-8

Book 3 *Fractions, Decimals, Percentages, Ratio and Proportion, Key Stage 2, Years 5 and 6*
ISBN: 1-84190-048-6

Book 4 *Solving Maths Word Problems*
ISBN: 1-84190-052-4

Book 6 *Improving the Plenary Session, Key Stage 2, Years 3 and 4*
ISBN: 1-84190-077-X

Book 7 *Improving the Plenary Session, Key Stage 2, Years 5 and 6*
ISBN: 1-84190-078-8

# Contents

# Introduction

According to Ofsted's report *The National Numeracy Strategy: An Interim Evaluation by HMI*, the plenary is the 'least successful element of the daily Maths lesson'. HMI stated that a typical problem was 'poor time management in the other elements of the lesson which meant that the time originally allocated to the plenary was lost.' The report stressed that the best plenary sessions are used to 'draw together the key ideas of the lesson, reinforce teaching points made earlier, assess what has been understood and correct errors and misconceptions.'

The plenary is designed to round off the maths lesson, with the class coming together as a whole. It should take between 10 and 15 minutes. Initially, you may have to make a big effort to make adequate time for a plenary. However, it soon becomes second nature.

This book focuses on how to improve the plenary part of your numeracy lessons. It gives basic lesson ideas, based on objectives from the National Numeracy Strategy's Framework for Teaching Mathematics. These will need developing and differentiating to suit your particular class. Each lesson idea comes with detailed suggestions for a suitable plenary session.

There are many ways in which the plenary part of the maths lesson can be executed. Here are some suggestions, most of which will be expanded on in this book:

- Ask the children to present and explain their work.
- Celebrate success in the children's work.
- Discuss what was the easiest/hardest/most enjoyable part of the lesson.
- Make a note of any successes and/or misconceptions to be dealt with at the time or during the next lesson. If common misconceptions are discovered during the lesson, it might be helpful to shorten the lesson and increase the plenary time to deal with these.
- Mark a written exercise done individually during the lesson, so that you can question the children appropriately and assess their work.
- Discuss and compare the efficiency of children's methods of working out a calculation.
- Help the children to generalise a rule from examples generated by different groups.
- Draw together what has been learned; reflect on what was important in the lesson; summarise key facts, ideas and vocabulary and what needs to be remembered.
- Play a fun game relevant to the maths learnt during the lesson.
- At the end of a unit of work, draw together what has been learnt over a series of lessons.
- Link skills that have been learned to problem solving within a context relevant to the children.

- ✪ Discuss what pupils will do next as a progression from the present lesson.
- ✪ Consolidate and develop what has been learnt. For example, if the lesson was about numbers on a number square, review the objectives and develop them further, extending the activity with larger numbers.
- ✪ Make links to work in other maths topics or other subjects.
- ✪ Set homework or a challenge to be done out of class.

**It must be stressed that each activity needs to be related to the objective of the lesson.**

Variety is essential. The same type of plenary will soon become tedious for both yourself and the children. It is therefore important that different aspects are covered during each week. All sessions, of course, will involve assessment of varying degrees.

There are a few important things to remember:

- ✪ Have a clear plan in mind of what you want to achieve during the plenary.
- ✪ Make sure you leave enough time for it.
- ✪ Ensure that the children know if they are to present something during the plenary, so that they can prepare for it.
- ✪ At the end of the plenary make a general evaluation of the lesson's success and how the children have worked.
- ✪ Have a definite routine at the end of a lesson to mark its finish, this is particularly relevant for the younger children.

# Topics and objectives

**Chapter 1 Presentation and explanation of the children's work**
Ideas for plenary sessions that give selected groups of children opportunities for showing and explaining their work to the rest of the class, based on lesson ideas which have the following objectives:

*Year 1 objectives:*
Count reliably at least 20 objects.
Count on and back in ones from a given number.
Use the vocabulary of comparing and ordering ordinal numbers.
Understand the process of addition by combining sets to make a total.
Use own mental strategies to solve simple story problems set in real life.
Know the days of the week.
Use everyday language to describe features of familiar 3-D and 2-D shapes.
Use everyday language to describe position, direction and movement.

*Year 2 objectives:*
Count from 0 or 1 in steps of two to 40 or more.
Compare two given numbers, say which is more or less and give a number lying between them.
Recognise and find simple fractions.
Add or subtract a multiple of 10 to or from a two-digit number, without crossing 100.
Read a simple scale to the nearest labelled division.
Make estimates and check using a simple timer.
Recognise and sketch a line of symmetry.
Solve a given problem by collecting, sorting and organising information in simple ways.

**Chapter 2 Progression - where are we going next?**
Ideas for plenary sessions which will highlight where the work the children have been doing will lead for the next lesson, based on lesson ideas which have the following objectives:

*Year 1 objectives:*
Describe and extend number sequences, what number comes next.
Understand and use the vocabulary of estimation and approximation.
Understand that two or more numbers can be added together.
Understand the operation of subtraction and related vocabulary.
Explain and record how a problem was solved.
Suggest suitable non-uniform units to estimate or measure length.
Describe and classify common 2-D shapes according to their properties.
Solve a given problem by collecting, sorting and organising information.

*Year 2 objectives:*
Recognise familiar multiples.
Understand and use the vocabulary of estimation and approximation.
Recognise and draw simple fractions of shapes.
Understand multiplication as describing an array.
Understand the operation of division as sharing, and associated vocabulary.
Explain methods and reasoning to solve problems, writing a number sentence.
Know the order of the months and seasons.
Recognise corners of doors are right angles, and that squares and rectangles have right angles at corners.

## Chapter 3 Links to other maths topics and curriculum areas

| | |
|---|---|
| Numeracy and literacy: | Year 1 |
| | Year 2 |
| Numeracy and science: | Growing plants |
| | Sorting and using materials |
| | Health and growth |
| Numeracy and history: | Homes |
| | Seaside holidays |
| | Florence Nightingale |
| Numeracy and geography: | Around our school |
| | Where in the world is Barnaby Bear? |
| Numeracy and art: | Mother Nature, designer |
| | What is sculpture? |

Numeracy and PE
Other areas of maths

## Chapter 4 Problem solving and games
Visualising
Acting out problems
Making up problems
Two-step problems
Games

## Chapter 5 Other ideas for an effective plenary
Discuss the easiest, hardest, most enjoyable part of the lesson
Identifying misconceptions
Generalising rules
Reflection, summarising and consolidation
Celebrating success

# Chapter 1

# Presentation and explanation of the children's work

When the National Numeracy Strategy was first put into place in primary schools, many teachers felt that this aspect of the lesson was not really important. In a lot of cases there was no time left for it at the end of the lesson, or if there was, the plenary consisted of a quick 'let's see what this group have done today' or the show and tell approach.

In my observations of lessons I still meet with teachers who say such things as:

"I don't want to stop the children when they are working so hard."
"Oh dear, I ran out of time."
"I'm not very good at plenaries, so I tend not to do them."

Happily, I meet far more teachers these days who are increasingly seeing the importance and value of the plenary part of the lesson, and use it confidently with a valid purpose.

**At the beginning of the plenary it is always important to refer to the objectives of the lesson. If you are using the explaining and presenting approach, the selected group of children/pairs/individuals will need to be able to tell the other children in the class what they have been doing, how it has helped them understand or has reinforced the objectives from the main teaching activity and whether they feel they have been successful.**

It can be counter-productive to ask the children to explain what they have been doing and how they got on during the plenary without prior warning. Doing so can cause embarrassment and anxiety in some children. It can also lack focus and quite frankly be a waste of ten minutes. The children need to be told in advance that they will be asked to talk about their work and how it has helped them achieve the lesson objectives, so that they can be prepared.

If you have a teaching assistant, it might be worth considering asking them to help the group they are working with to plan their plenary activity The teaching assistant does not necessarily need to work with the less able group always. Remember that it is the teacher's responsibility to teach that group at least once or twice a week. On these occasions you might ask your assistant to work with other children to help them with their presentation skills. Some children will welcome this help, as presenting and explaining work without a real focus can be very daunting to some, even the most able.

It is helpful to have a selection of appropriate questions that you might ask the children during the plenary, for example:

✪ What activity have you been doing during this session?
✪ Can you explain why you have been doing this?
✪ Has it helped you achieve the objectives?
✪ What do you know now that you didn't before?

# Year 1

### 1. Counting

> **Objective:** Count reliably at least 20 objects
> **Strand:** Numbers and the number system
> **Topic:** Counting, properties of numbers and number sequences

### *Group activity*

Counting sets of objects, matching with written numbers and recording their results.

Demonstrate the group activity by drawing circles on the board with shapes inside them.
Ask the children to count the shapes.
Give the children photocopiable sheet 1.
Ask the children to write the number of the shapes beside the circles.
Suggest that the children choose another number, draw the correct shapes and write the number beside them.

### *Plenary*

Refer to the objectives! Choose three groups of three or four children. Give each selected group a bag or box with a different number of objects inside; use mixed objects for the more able children. Each group takes it in turns to show the rest of the class how many objects are in their bag. They should explain to the class how they found their total, i.e. the last number that they counted tells them the number of objects that they have. Finally, ask all the children to help order the bags from smallest number of objects to largest. You could record this on the board for them.

### *Example*

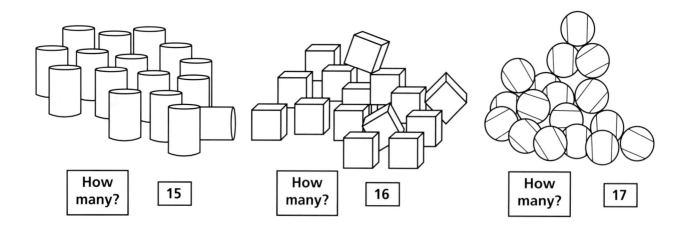

| How many? | 15 |

| How many? | 16 |

| How many? | 17 |

After you have done this, ask the children questions such as, 'How many more has the biggest group than the smallest?' 'How many more do we need to add to the group to make 20?'

## 2. Counting on and counting back

> **Objective:** Count on and back in ones from a given number
> **Strand:** Numbers and the number system
> **Topic:** Counting, properties of numbers and number sequences

### Paired activity
Counting on in ones from a given number using a number line.

Begin by looking at two different types of number line (not just a straight one). Ask the children to come and show everyone where different numbers are. Show them a number line with missing numbers and ask the children to tell you what the missing numbers are and how they know.

Give each pair of children an A3 number line, such as the one on photocopiable sheet 2. Their first job is to fill in the missing numbers. (They may need a completed number line to refer to.) They need coloured cubes and dice. Place a cube on the number 1. Take it in turns to throw the dice and count on the number shown. Colour the circle. Record: (if 4 thrown) 1 + 4 = 5. Throw again, move on that number, colour and record, for example 5 + 2 = 7 (if 2 thrown). See how far along the number line they can get. This is an activity that can easily be differentiated (by size of number line) to suit the needs of your class.

### Plenary
Refer to the objectives! Make sure that you have both a number line and a number square available for the children to demonstrate on and markers that can be attached to them using Blutak. Ask the selected children to come to the front and show everybody what they did using some examples of their work, ensuring that they explain as they do it. Finish off by choosing some random numbers for everyone to help count on, in ones, a number thrown by the dice. Choose other children to put markers on the number line, for example:

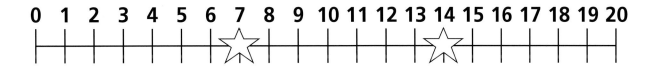

What is one more than 6?

What is 6 more than 8?

Repeat with larger numbers on the number square.

---

## 3. Ordering ordinal numbers

**Objective:** Use the vocabulary of comparing and ordering ordinal numbers
**Strand:** Numbers and the number system
**Topic:** Place value and ordering

### *Group activity*
Ordering pictures from 1st to 10th (up to 20th for more able children) and making up a story to go with their ordering.

To demonstrate, choose three children to mime a hopping race. Ask which child came first, second and third. Choose five more to help. They will mime a jumping race. Ask which positions they came in. Now choose ten children. Give them a position card. Stand them in a line. Make up a story to do with a race and as the children 'finish', ask the others to position them correctly.
Give each group an activity similar to the one below. Photocopy the cards on photocopiable sheets 3 and 4 and give a set to each group.

### *Who came first?*
Ask each group to cut out the ten animals and put them in order from first to last. Ask them to label them (1st, 2nd, 3rd, 4th, 5th, 6th, 7th, 8th, 9th, 10th) and make up a story about what they have been doing.
Explain to the selected group that they will need to tell the rest of the class their story during the plenary.

### *Plenary*
Refer to the objectives! The group then need to show how they ordered their animals and tell the class the story that they made up. If preferred they could act out their story using toy animals as their props.

## 4. Addition

**Objective:** Understand the process of addition by combining sets to make a total
**Strand:** Calculations
**Topic:** Understanding addition

### *Group activity*
Making sets of numbers of objects and totalling them

Demonstrate the following group activity, asking the children how they would find the total number.
Give each group some pieces of A3 paper with boxes and large circles drawn on them and up to 20 cubes, toys, counters or something similar. Ask them to put some objects in one of the circles and some in the other, write down the number in each box, then total them and finally record the answer.

*Example*

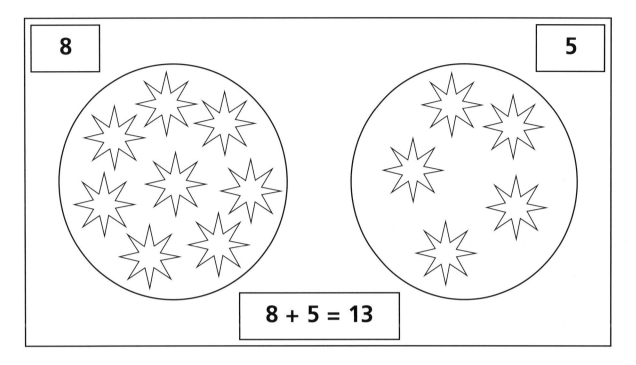

## *Plenary*

Refer to the objectives! Supply one of the selected group with hoops or something similar. Ask them to put some objects in the hoops and demonstrate to the children how they found the total, explaining as clearly as they can, as shown in the example below.

**"I'm going to take the soldiers in this hoop and put them with the others and count them all up."**

**"I know that there are two soldiers here, so I'm now going to count on these four soldiers."**

## 5. Money problems

> **Objective:** Use own mental strategies to solve simple 'story' problems set in real life
> **Strand:** Solving problems
> **Topic:** Problems involving money

### *Group activity*

Answering money problems involving finding totals and giving change.

Demonstrate by trying a few visualising activities. Ask the children to listen carefully and follow your instructions:
"Close your eyes. Imagine you are holding a purse. It has some pennies in it. You count them. There are five: 1 2 3 4 5. Now you are putting another one in. How many are there?"
"Now you are taking two out. How many have you now?'
"Your mum gives you three more. How many have you got in your purse now?"
"You want to buy four penny sweets. Have you enough in your purse?"
"Buy them. How much have you got left now?"
Ask the children in their groups to make up a story like that and act it out with coins.

### *Plenary*

Refer to the objectives! Give the selected group a scenario to act out to the rest of the class.

### *Example*

"Tammy and her three friends went to the shop and bought five penny sweets each. How much did they spend altogether? If they gave the shopkeeper 20p, how much change would they receive?"
The group will need time to prepare their presentation during their group work session. Ask them to use the correct money during their 'scene' and any other appropriate props, for example a toy till, some pretend sweets.
The rest of the class need to describe what the scene is about and give the answers to the problem.

## 6. Days of the week

> **Objective:** Know the days of the week
> **Strand:** Measures
> **Topic:** Time

### *Group activity*

Ordering the days of the week and thinking of something special that happens on each one.

Begin the lesson by singing the days of the week song. Talk about each day and ask the children what they do on each one, for example I go to Beavers on Monday, church on Sunday, PE on Thursday. Give each group some labels with the days of the week on.

Ask them to order the days and draw pictures to show themselves doing something special for each day.

*Plenary*
Refer to the objectives! Ask the selected group to tell the rest of the class how they ordered the days (maybe by reminding themselves through the song) and to talk about the things they do on each of the days.
Finish by singing the song again.

## 7. 2-D and 3-D shapes

**Objective:** Use everyday language to describe features of familiar 3-D and 2-D shapes
**Strand:** Shape and space
**Topic:** Properties of 3-D and 2-D shapes

### Group activity
Sorting shapes, with the children deciding the criteria.

Prepare a grid like the one below. Demonstrate to the children what you want them to do by showing them a selection of 2-D or 3-D shapes.

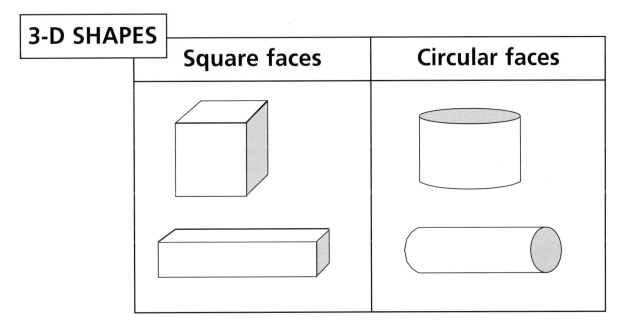

Put your shape in the appropriate section of the grid, discussing with the children which section is correct. Ask what other criteria you could have used, for example straight edges, hollow or solid. Give each group some 2-D or 3-D shapes or boxes and ask them to make up their own criteria for sorting them. Provide them with a blank grid.

### Plenary
Refer to the objectives! Give each group a selection of shapes. Ask them to look carefully at each one and then group them according to the criteria they used for their group activities. Give the children two or three minutes to do this. Choose two groups, or more if you have time and invite them to explain to the whole class how they sorted their particular shapes.

## 8. Position

**Objective:** Use everyday language to describe position, direction and movement
**Strand:** Shape and space
**Topic:** Position and direction

### *Paired activity*
Matching pictures and words

Begin by demonstrating the vocabulary that you want to focus on during the lesson, showing the words on card.
Give each pair a copy of photocopiable sheet 5 and ask them to match the words to the pictures. If there is time they could record what they have done by drawing their own pictures and writing the appropriate label.

### *Plenary*
Refer to the objectives! Ask the selected group to tell the class which word they matched with which picture and why. Then ask them to demonstrate what they have learnt in a practical way. Do this by giving each child in the group an object and whisper a position to each child. In turns, the children demonstrate the position, i.e. over, under, on, in, in front, behind. The rest of the class need to work out which one is being demonstrated.

# Year 2

### 9. Two-step counting

**Objective:** Count from 0 or 1 in steps of two to 40 or more
**Strand:** Numbers and the number system
**Topic:** Counting, properties of numbers and number sequences

### *Paired activity*
Counting sets of shapes or objects in twos.

Show the children a pile of cubes or counters (you will find this more effective if you use an OHP) and ask them how they can find out how many there are:

> **Answers that you might get:**
>
> "I counted each one."
> "I saw the first 4 and counted
>   on from there."
> "I saw 4 and another 4 which makes
>   8 and then counted the rest."
> "I counted in 2's"

Discuss all the suggested methods and decide which is the most efficient. Aim towards counting in twos. Practise counting in twos from 0, 1, 2, 5, 10.

Give the children a copy of photocopiable sheet 6 to work on with a partner. Ask them to estimate how many dots they think there are before counting. One counts first and the other checks. Were they close to their estimates?

## *Plenary*

Refer to the objectives! Ask some pairs of children to tell everyone what they have been doing – estimating the dots, counting in twos, checking and deciding if their estimates were close to the real amount. Put some more cubes or counters on the OHP. Ask the pairs to demonstrate what they did using these cubes.

## 10. Place value and ordering

> **Objective:** Compare two given numbers, say which is more or less and give a number lying between them
> **Strand:** Numbers and the number system
> **Topic:** Place value and ordering

### *Group activity*
Comparing numbers

Begin by writing some numbers on the board, for example 43, 36, 63, 38, 45, 54, 41, 46, 50. Ask the class such questions as "Which is less 36 or 63? Why?"; "Which is the greatest 45 or 54? Why?"; "What numbers lie between 38 and 43?"; "Which number is closest to 46 ….. 41 or 50?" Give each group a selection of number cards and three instruction cards. See photocopiable sheets 7 and 8.

### *Plenary*
Refer to the objectives! Ask the selected group to tell the others which number cards they used and write them on the board. One of the group should then tell everybody the instructions they were given one at a time and the others should explain what they did and how they got their answers.

Finish by asking the group a few questions along the lines of: Which number is closest to 40:37 or 44?"; "Which number is closest to 52:56 or 49?" Ask them to explain how they knew.

This is one area where many children fail in KS1 SATs: they tend to look at the initial digit and make a decision based on that, i.e. 56 is closest to 50 because of the 5.

## 11. Fractions

**Objective:** Recognise and find simple fractions
**Strand:** Numbers and the number system
**Topic:** Fractions

### Group activity
Finding a half and a quarter of amounts of cubes and counters.

Begin by demonstrating halves and quarters, practically with numbers and objects placed in different arrays, for example:

1. Amy ate $\frac{1}{4}$ of these chocolate buttons. (Place 8 chocolate buttons in a circle.)

How many did she eat?

2. Kieran ate $\frac{1}{2}$ of these biscuits. (Place 10 biscuits in 3 rows of 4, 4, 2)

How many did he eat?

3. Tom gave away $\frac{1}{4}$ of these marbles. (Place 12 marbles in 2 rows of 6.)

How many did he give away?

If you have a Velcro board, the children could come to the front to work these out, actually taking the 'chocolate buttons', 'biscuits' and 'marbles' on and off, so that the whole class can see what is going on. This makes for a very effective demonstration. Give the groups of children some cubes and instruction cards, for example:

| Put 8 cubes here. | Put 12 cubes here. | Put 16 cubes here. |
|---|---|---|
| | | |
| **How many is $\frac{1}{4}$?** | **How many is $\frac{1}{2}$?** | **How many is $\frac{1}{2}$?** |

### Plenary
Refer to the objectives! Ask the selected group to demonstrate their work. They could use the OHP, placing the cubes on it and grouping them into quarters or halves.
To finish, give them 12 cubes and ask them to tell you how many $\frac{1}{4}$ would be, then $\frac{2}{4}$ and $\frac{3}{4}$.
Ask them if they can tell you what other fraction is the same as $\frac{2}{4}$.

## 12. Mental calculations

> **Objective:** Add or subtract a multiple of 10 to or from a two-digit number, without crossing 100
> **Strand:** Calculations
> **Topic:** Mental calculation strategies (+ and -)

### Paired activity
Adding multiples of 10 using a number square.

Begin by showing the children a large number square. See photocopiable sheet 9.
Ask the children to find certain numbers (an even number, a number between 20 and 30, a number that is more than 6 but less than 15, a multiple of 10 and so on) and put a marker such as a sticky star on the number.

Make sure each pair of children has a number square, counters or markers, digit cards, a die and + and – cards to use. See photocopiable sheet 10.
The children should randomly pick two digit cards and make up a 2-digit number, then pick either a + or – card.
They then place their counter or marker on the 2-digit number on the number square.
Next, they throw the dice to show the number of tens they will either add or take away.
They make the calculation and put another counter or marker on that square.
They repeat this as many times as possible in the time allowed, trying to cover as many of the squares as they can. They could record their work, e.g. 56 + 30 = 86. If their numbers take them above 100, allow them to try to find the answer. If they take them below 1, they simply pick again.

### Plenary
Refer to the objectives! Ask some of the pairs of children to report back to the others, by demonstrating what they did using the class number square and markers. Make sure they explain why they did what they did.

## 13. Measuring with a metre stick

> **Objective:** Read a simple scale to the nearest labelled division
> **Strand:** Measures
> **Topic:** Length, mass and capacity

### Group activity
Measuring to the nearest 10 centimetres

Demonstrate, inviting children to help you, the measuring of a variety of objects with a metre stick. Then demonstrate measuring smaller items using strips of card that are 10 centimetres long, rounding the measurements to the nearest 10 centimetres. Repeat this using a metre stick, comparing the 10 centimetre labelled divisions with your strips of card. During the group work, ask the children to measure items of their choice (have some strategically placed around the room!) to the nearest 10 centimetres and record.

## Plenary

Refer to the objectives! Ask the selected group to demonstrate how they measured their items using a metre stick. Then ask them to measure some items that you have chosen, for example a book, chair, whiteboard, table, toy box. They need to demonstrate and explain how they would find out their heights to the nearest 10 centimetres. This could be an opportunity to introduce the word 'approximately' even though it is part of the Year 3 vocabulary.

## 14. Time

> **Objective:** Make estimates and check using a simple timer
> **Strand:** Measures
> **Topic:** Time

## Group activity

Making estimates of how long it takes for someone to do something and then checking with a one-minute sand timer.

Begin by discussing how long a minute is. Use a one-minute timer, ask the children to sit very still and quietly until the sand runs through. Did it seem a long time?
Invite a volunteer to come to the front to do some jumping. Ask the class to estimate how many jumps they will be able to do in one minute. Check by timing the volunteer. Find out who made the closest estimate.
Now ask a volunteer to take their shoes and socks off and then put them back on again. Ask the rest of the class to estimate how many minutes it will take, check and find out who was closest.
Ask the children to work in groups of four and provide them with a timer and instruction cards, such as those on photocopiable sheet 11.

## Plenary

Refer to the objectives! Ask the selected group to choose one of their activities to demonstrate to the rest of the class.
They will need to 'act' out exactly what they did: the reading of the instructions, deciding who would to do the activity, who would time, making the estimates, checking by timing and discussing how close their estimates were.
After this, ask the others in the class to choose one of the children in the group to do something that they suggest and repeat the procedure as demonstrated.

## 15. Line symmetry

> **Objective:** Recognise and sketch a line of symmetry
> **Strand:** Shape and space
> **Topic:** Line symmetry

### Group activity
Looking at a selection of pictures and sketching lines of symmetry.
Begin by demonstrating lines of symmetry on pictures using an OHP and acetates.
Flags, road signs, insects and shapes are good examples to use.
Ask the children where they think the line or lines of symmetry are and why. Then draw them onto each acetate.
Give each group a selection of pictures and ask them to sort them into three groups: those with no symmetry, those with one line and those with more than one line. Ask them to draw the lines of symmetry onto each picture. See photocopiable sheets 12 and 13.

### Plenary
Refer to the objectives! Ask the selected group to explain what is meant by symmetry, using their sorted pictures as visual aids.

## 16. Solving problems with data handling

> **Objective:** Solve a given problem by collecting, sorting and organising information in simple ways
> **Strand:** Handling data
> **Topic:** Organising and using data

### Group activity
Collecting, sorting and organising the information necessary to solve a given problem.

This should take place after two or three whole-class lessons on handling data, so that the children are well practised at collecting data, knowing how to display it on a simple block graph and finding the information from it to answer questions.
In Chapter 2 (Year 1 section) you will find a great activity for introducing handling data.
Give each group a problem to solve for example:
"What do six- and seven-year-olds like to drink?"
"What is the most popular board game among six- and seven-year-olds?"
"Which sport do six- and seven-year-olds like best?"
They should then tackle the problem in the way you have taught them to in previous whole-class teaching sessions. It would be a good idea to give them questions to answer on card, such as the examples given overleaf.

**Drinks:**
What do most children like to drink?
Why do you think this is?
How many children did you ask?

**Board games:**
What do most children like to play?
What is the least popular game?
Why do you think this is?
How many children did you ask?

**Sport:**
What sports were chosen?
Which was the most popular?
How many voted for that?
How many children did you ask?

### *Plenary*
Refer to the objectives! Ask each group to feed back, using your questions as prompts.
Make up a problem from all their work for them to solve, for example:
"Our class is going to have a fun day next week. In the morning we will be playing great
Numeracy and Literacy games. In the afternoon we will be playing some games, two types
of board games and two types of sport. In between activities, I will make everyone a
drink. How can we use all the information that you have collected to help us decide what
games we will play and what drink I will make?"
This will make a purposeful end to the session (especially if you do organise a 'fun day')
as the children can draw conclusions from the information they have gathered during
their group work.

# Photocopiable Sheet 1
# Counting

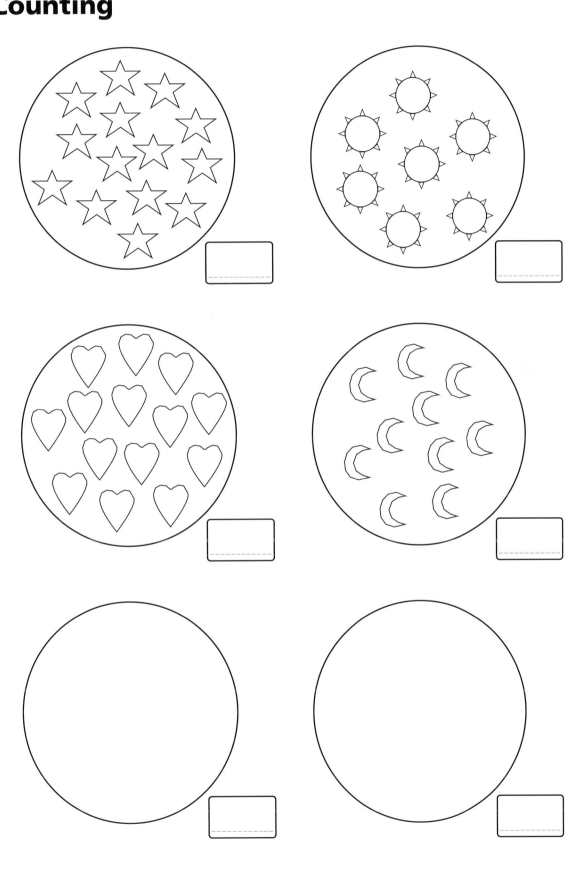

# Photocopiable Sheet 2
# Counting on and back

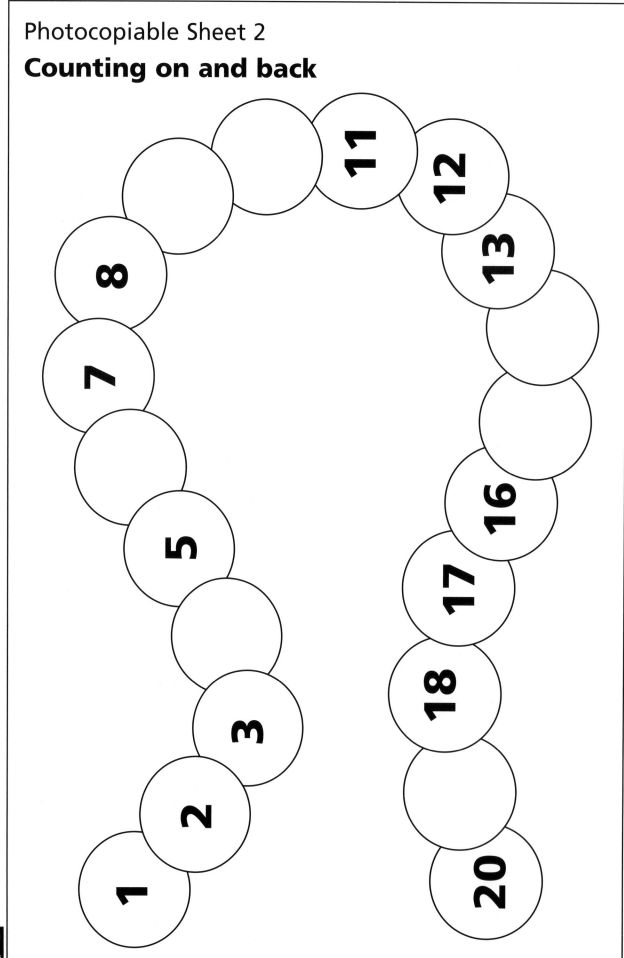

# Photocopiable Sheet 3
# **Ordering ordinal numbers A**

Photocopiable Sheet 4

# Ordering ordinal numbers B

| | | | | |
|---|---|---|---|---|
| **1ˢᵗ** | **2ⁿᵈ** | **3ʳᵈ** | **4ᵗʰ** | **5ᵗʰ** |
| **6ᵗʰ** | **7ᵗʰ** | **8ᵗʰ** | **9ᵗʰ** | **10ᵗʰ** |

# Photocopiable Sheet 5
## Position

| | |
|---|---|
| **In front** | **Behind** | **On** |
| **In** | **Over** | **Under** |

## Photocopiable Sheet 6
# Counting in twos

## How Many?
## Count in 2's

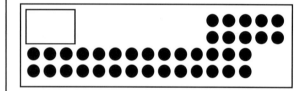 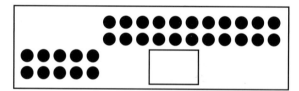

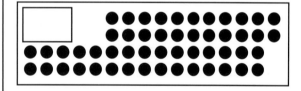 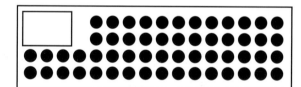

Make up some dotty boxes for
your friend to count in 2's.

Photocopiable Sheet 7

# Ordering cardinal numbers A

| | | |
|---|---|---|
| 64 | 12 | 19 |
| 46 | 78 | 91 |
| 21 | 53 | 54 |
| 35 | 87 | 45 |

Photocopiable Sheet 8

# Ordering cardinal numbers B

Order your number cards from smallest to largest.
Write them down in order.

Sort your cards into 2 piles, one pile for numbers less than 50 and another for those that are more than 50.

Choose the 4 cards that are closest to 50.
Write them down.

Work out how many numbers they are away from 50.
Write the answers beside your 4 numbers.

Pick all the cards that have a 4 in.
Order them from smallest to greatest.
Write them down.

Think ofas many other 2-digit numbers that have a 4 in as possible.
Write them down. How many?

Photocopiable Sheet 9
# Mental calculations A

| 1 | 2 | 3 | 4 | 5 | 6 | 7 | 8 | 9 | 10 |
|---|---|---|---|---|---|---|---|---|---|
| 11 | 12 | 13 | 14 | 15 | 16 | 17 | 18 | 19 | 20 |
| 21 | 22 | 23 | 24 | 25 | 26 | 27 | 28 | 29 | 30 |
| 31 | 32 | 33 | 34 | 35 | 36 | 37 | 38 | 39 | 40 |
| 41 | 42 | 43 | 44 | 45 | 46 | 47 | 48 | 49 | 50 |
| 51 | 52 | 53 | 54 | 55 | 56 | 57 | 58 | 59 | 60 |
| 61 | 62 | 63 | 64 | 65 | 66 | 67 | 68 | 69 | 70 |
| 71 | 72 | 73 | 74 | 75 | 76 | 77 | 78 | 79 | 80 |
| 81 | 82 | 83 | 84 | 85 | 86 | 87 | 88 | 89 | 90 |
| 91 | 92 | 93 | 94 | 95 | 96 | 97 | 98 | 99 | 100 |

# Photocopiable Sheet 10
# **Mental calculations B**

| | |
|:---:|:---:|
| **−** | **0** |

| | | |
|:---:|:---:|:---:|
| **1** | **2** | **3** |
| **4** | **5** | **6** |
| **7** | **8** | **9** |

| |
|:---:|
| **+** |

# Photocopiable Sheet 11
# Time

## How many hops a minute?
**Estimate**
Names of children and estimates

**Time them**
Results

**How close were you?**

## How many times can you write your name in a minute?
**Estimate**
Names of children and estimates

**Time them**
Results

**How close were you?**

## How long does it take to change for PE?
**Estimate**
Names of children and estimates

**Time them**
Results

**How close were you?**

# Photocopiable Sheet 12
# Line symmetry A

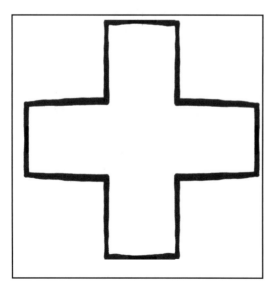

# Photocopiable Sheet 13
## Line symmetry B

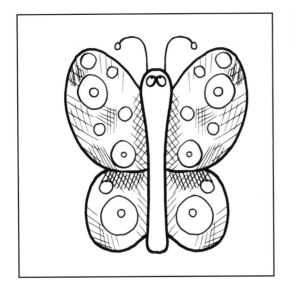

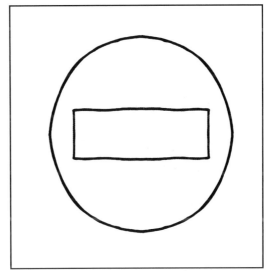

# Chapter 2
# Progression – where are we going next?

Put yourself inside the mind of a young child who has been asked to estimate a number of items. Their immediate reaction will probably be to think:

✪ I want to count them to find out exactly how many there are.
✪ I can count: why should I guess and maybe get it wrong?
✪ What is the point of estimating?
✪ I think I'll count and hope the teacher doesn't see me!

Does this sound familiar?

Estimating is a very good example of why it is important that the children know the purpose of what they are doing and where it will lead in the future. Estimating is a useful skill if the children need to know numbers and measurements in a practical context, for example:

✪ Will there be enough potatoes in this bag for our family to eat this Sunday?
✪ Will I have enough pennies to go to the shop to buy some sweets?

Estimating the answer first, answering and comparing the answer to the estimate is also important for calculation work. If they are close, the answer is likely to be correct and it will be worth a proper check.

This is the same in all areas of maths. It is important that the children know the 'whole picture' of what they are learning and why, so that they can see that it is relevant to them. Children always learn best if they can see why they are doing something. On occasions, during your plenary, tell the children how what they have learnt will help them during the next lesson.

This chapter aims to give lesson objectives from the NNS Framework for Teaching Mathematics, lesson ideas and a plenary outlining where the work the children have been doing will lead for the next lesson.

**Remember to refer to the objective of the lesson taught initially and then inform the children of what they will be doing next time and why.**

# Year 1

### 1. Number sequences

> **Objective:** Describe and extend number sequences, what number comes next
> **Leading to:** Fill in the missing numbers
> **Strand:** Numbers and the number system
> **Topic:** Counting, properties of numbers and number sequences

## Group activity
Looking at number sequences.

Begin by working with a number line. Ask the children to point to different numbers on it. Ask them to count to 20 and back. Then count on and back from numbers you specify. Give the groups number strings and a number line each, such as the example on photocopiable sheet 14. Ask them to circle the three given numbers and the three that have been 'boxed' on to the number line.

## Plenary
Ask the children to feed back what they did during their activities. Tell them that now they have succeeded in achieving this part of the objective, during the next lesson they will be able to move on and work out more complicated sequences involving missing numbers in a string of numbers. Put some examples on the board, e.g.

| | | | | |
|---|---|---|---|---|
| 2 | ☐ | ☐ | 8 | 10 |
| ☐ | ☐ | 9 | ☐ | 3 |

## 2. Estimating

> **Objective:** Understand and use the vocabulary of estimation and approximation, and give a sensible estimate for a number of objects, up to 30
> **Leading to:** Estimating whether there is enough
> **Strand:** Numbers and the number system
> **Topic:** Estimating and rounding

## Group activity
Estimating numbers in a range of practical contexts.

Begin by displaying various numbers of small cubes on the OHP or larger ones on a tray. The children need to estimate how many cubes there are on view. They must not count, so ask them to close their eyes, then display the cubes and ask the children to have a look. Give them a few seconds before you hide the display.
Ask the children for their estimates. When they have given an estimate, ask them to tell you why they thought as they did.
As a group activity, give the children a pile of cards with a different number of shapes on. See photocopiable sheet 15. One member of the group needs to show a card for a few seconds so that the others do not have time to count. The others need to make an estimate and write it down on paper.
They then compare their estimates and the 'shower' counts the number of shapes. They then find out who is the closest. Give the 'winner' a counter. Do this several times, each child taking it in turns to be a 'shower'. Find out who is the most accurate estimator, i.e. the one with the most counters:

## Plenary
Discuss what the children have been doing. Ask them whether they found that, as their attempts increased, their estimates became more accurate. Tell the children that as they have achieved this objective, during their next lesson they will be using their work from today to help make practical estimates such as: "Are there enough chairs for these children?"; "Are there enough pencils for these books?". Try an example with the children.
Expect 'yes' or 'no' answers. Once they have been given, check. Are there too many or too few? How many more or less to make them match?

## 3. Addition

> **Objective:** Understand that two or more numbers can be added together
> **Leading to:** Finding three numbers that give a given number
> **Strand:** Calculations
> **Topic:** Understanding addition

### Group activity
Getting children to respond to oral questions and explain the strategy they have used.

Begin by asking the children to add up two numbers that you call out: 3 + 2, 6 + 2, 5 + 4, and so on. Ask the children how they worked their answer out. Some of their answers may surprise you! For example, when explaining how they tackled 3 + 2, children may say:

"I doubled three and took one off."
"I doubled two and added one more."
"I put three in my head and counted on two more."
"I just know that 3 + 2 is 5."
"I used my fingers because I have three here and two here and that's all on one hand."

Next extend this to three numbers.
For their group work, give each group a pile of cards with different calculations.
They take a card and each member of the group has to suggest a different way of totalling the numbers. Ask the children to try to record these in any way they can so that they can tell the rest of the class about their work during the plenary.

### Example
**5 + 4 + 1**

I know that:
"4 + 1 = 5, 5 + 5 = 10"
"5 + 4 = 9, 9 + 1 = 10"
"5 +1 = 6, 6 + 4 = 10, because I know my number bonds."

### Plenary
Spend some time taking examples of the children's work and listening to their strategies. Next, tell the children that as they have worked so hard and achieved today's objective, next time they will be thinking of three different numbers to make a given total, for example "What three numbers will make 12?"
Work through this problem with the children. Write the number up and brainstorm around it, for example:

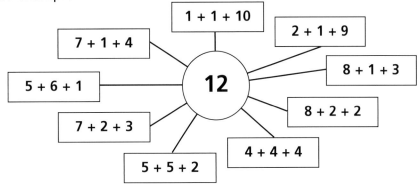

## 4. Subtraction

> **Objective:** Understand the operation of subtraction and the related vocabulary
> **Leading to:** Understanding that addition can help with subtraction as they are inverse operations.
> **Strand:** Calculations
> **Topic:** Understanding subtraction

### *Group activity*

Understanding that subtraction is also taking away and finding the difference between.

Begin by asking the children what they think the word subtraction means. Hopefully some of them will remember! Give some practical examples of this, involving children and apparatus:
**Taking away:** One child has five cubes; another takes away three. How many are left? Imagine five sweets. You eat two. How many are left?
**Finding the difference between:** Ask six children to stand together as a group and four children to stand together as another group. Ask the rest of the children to tell you what the difference is between the two groups. Allow them to give all kinds of answers such as "There are more boys in that group"; "They have dark hair and the others don't". Eventually, someone will say that there are two more children in the first group. It is important that the children talk about all the differences, before they are focused onto the one related to subtraction.
For the group activity, give each group a pile of cards with different numbers of dots on. See photocopiable sheet 16. The group picks two at a time and has to work out the difference between them. Demonstrate first.

### *Plenary*

Discuss some of the children's calculations. Then explain to the children that another way of taking away is to say "how many more to make ..." This links with addition. Tell the children that during the next lesson they will be using addition to help them take away. Give them some examples of this:
"If we want to know what to add on to 6 to make 10, what do we do?" A possible answer may be to put up six fingers and then count how many more must be put up to make ten. "Therefore 4 + 6 = 10." Explain that another way of doing this could be to say: "We have 10. Everyone put up 10 fingers. We know that we have to add something onto 6 to get this, so if we take 6 fingers down, what we are left with is the missing number." Write the two equations on the board: $6 + 4 = 10$ and $10 - 6 = 4$.
Ask the children what they notice. Repeat with another example from the group work.

## 5. Word problems

> **Objective:** Explain and record how the problem was solved
> **Leading to:** Making up their own number stories
> **Strand:** Solving problems
> **Topic:** Making decisions

## Group activity
Solving simple word problems, explaining them and recording their reasoning.

Demonstrate the activity by working through some problems as a class:
"There are 26 children here today. I only have 23 pencils. How many more pencils do I need, so that you all have one to work with?"
Ask the class to tell you what the important facts are, what the question is and how they will answer it.
Give the groups some problem cards and sheets of paper and pens. Ask them to work out the answers by thinking in the way you demonstrated and recording in a way they will be able to tell you about.

## Plenary
Discuss what the children have been doing in their groups, taking an example from each. Continue by telling the children that during the next lesson they will be making up number stories or problems of their own, from numbers that you will be giving them.

## Examples
$3 + 4 = 7$
"I had 3 grapes. Mum gave me 7 more so now I have 7."
"Sue gave me 3 crayons. I found 4 more. How many do I have now?"

$\boxed{\phantom{000}} - 6 = 2$
"I lost 6 Beanie Babies. Now I've only got 2. How many did I start with?"
"Benji had 2 raisins. He had eaten 6. How many did he have to begin with?"

## 6. Measuring

> **Objective:** Suggest suitable non-uniform units to estimate or measure length
> **Leading to:** Suggest standard units to estimate or measure length
> **Strand:** Measures
> **Topic:** Length, mass and capacity

## Group activity
Suggest things that could be used to measure a variety of objects.

Begin by telling the children that they will be finding things that could be measured using rulers, matchsticks, small garden canes and metre sticks. Show them a selection of classroom objects and ask them to help you sort them into groups – those that can be measured by the measuring items you have.

Give the groups a selection of objects and four labelled sorting rings. Display the four types of measuring equipment for all to see and ask the children to sort their objects into the most sensible ring for their sizes.

*Plenary*

Ask the children to tell you in which ring they have put certain objects and why. Follow this up by telling the children that now they have achieved this objective, they will be looking at different items in the next lesson and deciding for themselves which standard unit they could use to measure them. The choices you could give them might be a centimetre cube, 10cm strip of card, 30cm ruler and a metre stick. Demonstrate by showing some items and the four standard measurements and asking their opinions on which would be the most suitable measures to use.

## 7. 2-D shapes

**Objective:** Describe and classify common 2-D shapes according to their properties
**Leading to:** Recognising hidden shapes by description or feel and naming them
**Strand:** Shape and space
**Topic:** Properties of 3-D and 2-D shapes

*Group activity*

Sorting 2-D shapes according to the following criteria: number of corners, straight sides, number of sides.

Begin by showing the class a variety of shapes and talking about their properties, asking such questions as: "How many sides has this shape?"; "Can you show me the sides?"; "Are there any corners?"; "Can you think what a shape must have if it has corners?". Give each group a selection of 2-D shapes and a grid for two criteria and ask them to sort their shapes according to the criteria set. They do not have to know the names of the shapes other than square, circle, rectangle and triangle:

*Example*

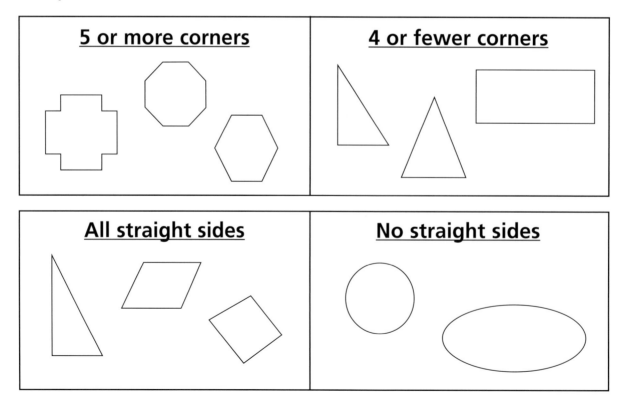

## Plenary

Discuss the shapes again by asking the children to describe as many properties as they can. Tell them that tomorrow, because they have done so well today, they will be deciding what the shapes are by feel or description alone, using the proper names. Demonstrate an example of this:
"My shape has 4 sides all the same length and 4 corners all the same size. What is it?"

## 8. Whole-class data handling

> **Objective:** Solve a given problem by collecting, sorting and organising information in simple ways, teacher led as a whole class
> **Leading to:** Solving a problem as above but unaided in small groups
> **Strand:** Handling Data
> **Topic:** Organising and using data

### Whole-class activity

Solve a problem as per the objective, discussing such questions as "How can we find out?"; "How can we organise the information?"; "Why might we need to know?"

Think of a problem relevant to your class, that needs solving, for instance:

During a literacy lesson your class might be involved with making up instructions for looking after pets, or thinking about pets to put in a pet shop. This could involve such a problem as: "Which pets should we include in our instruction book/pet shop?"
Ask the question, "How can we find out?"
The children will probably suggest finding out what pets the class have or would like to have, given the choice.
Do a 'post it' note graph-building activity, discussing and making up the vertical and horizontal axes labels and filling it with their choice of pets. Ask the children to contribute by adding the labels.
Have an outline graph prepared.
Decide as a class which pets you want to use.
Give each of the axes a title using two sticky notes labelled 'pets' and 'number of children'. Ask two children to add them to your outline graph. Label each section of the horizontal axis with the names of the pets and ask some children to stick the labels on.
Ask the children to draw the pet of their choice, from the class list, onto a sticky note and in turns add them to the graph.
Write numbers on sticky notes to add to the vertical axis.

### Plenary

Ask the class what this graph tells them. Ask them to ask you a question that you can answer from the graph. Ask them questions to promote their thinking for example, "How many children were asked?"; "Is there an animal that probably need not be included?"; "Do you think all the animals should be included? Why?".
Come to a conclusion regarding the pets that the class would like to see included.
Finish by telling the children that because they have learnt so much during this lesson, they will be working in groups tomorrow to solve problems that you will give them by themselves. Set the scene for the problem solving to come, and discuss it with the children, for example: "Mr Brown owns a farm. He has been asked to raise one type of animal for a children's farmyard, grow one type of fruit to sell at the local shop and to produce milk for one food to sell at the same shop. Mr Brown has got to decide which animal to raise, which fruit to grow and what to do with his milk. How can you help him?"
Give each group part of the problem.

# Year 2

## 9. Recognising multiples

> **Objective:** Recognise familiar multiples
> **Leading to:** Sorting multiples in 'Venn Diagram' type of display.
> **Strand:** Numbers and the number system
> **Topic:** Counting, properties of numbers and the number sequences

### Paired activity

Looking at 2-digit multiples of two, five and ten and recognising that they end with particular numbers.

Begin by counting in twos, fives and tens from zero up to 100. Ask the class what they can tell you about the numbers each time such as, multiples of two always end with zero, two, four, six or eight, multiples of five always end with zero or five, multiples of ten always end with zero.

Demonstrate the paired activity by writing on the board some mixed multiples of these numbers and ask the children to identify to which they belong, for example:
25 (5), 40 (2, 5, 10), 66 (2), 80 (2, 5, 10).

Provide pairs of children with a sheet of numbers similar to those shown below and ask them to identify the multiples (2, 5 or 10) of different numbers.

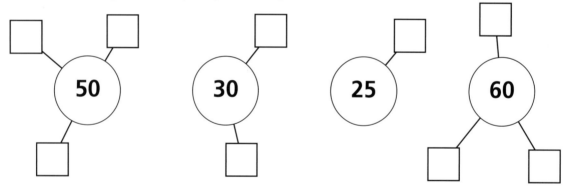

### Plenary

Discuss the results of the paired work. Tell the children that now they can recognise the multiples of two, five and ten, during the next lesson they will be given a larger selection of numbers to sort in a more complicated way, but one that tells them more information. They will need to sort the numbers into groups according to whether they are multiples of two, five, ten or a mixture. Show them an example on the board.

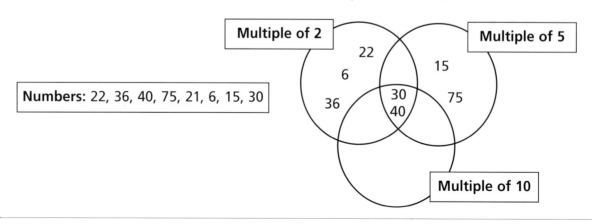

Numbers: 22, 36, 40, 75, 21, 6, 15, 30

Ask the children what they notice about the multiples of ten (they are all multiples of two and five as well). Tell them that they will be making similar conclusions about multiples of two and five.

### 10. Estimating position on a number line

> **Objectives:** Understand and use the vocabulary of estimation and approximation, give a sensible estimate for a number of objects and recording on a number lin.
> **Leading to:** Estimating the position of a point on a number line
> **Strand:** Numbers and the number system
> **Topic:** Estimating and rounding

#### *Group activity*
Recording estimates on a number line.

Begin by showing the children counters or cubes on an OHP and asking them to estimate how many are there. You do not want the children to have time to count the counters so start by asking the children to close their eyes. Display the counters or cubes and tell the children to look. Give them a few seconds and then turn off the OHP. Invite a few children to come to the front and mark their estimates on a number line from 0 to 40.

#### *Group activity*
Give each group some cards with different numbers of shapes on. One child needs to show a card for a few seconds, everyone makes an estimate and then plots their estimate on a number line similar to the one above.

#### *Plenary*
Discuss what the children have been doing, asking a few to give examples. Tell the children that during the next lesson they will be looking at cards on a number line from 1 to 50 and estimating the number represented by the card on the number line. Give examples like the one below.

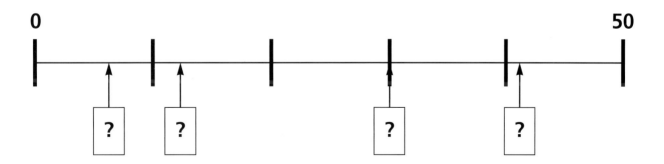

## 11. Fractions of shapes

> **Objective:** Recognise and draw simple fractions of shapes
> **Leading to:** Recognise what is not one half or one quarter and explain
> **Strand:** Numbers and the number system
> **Topic:** Fractions

### *Paired activity*
Recognising what fraction of a shape is shaded

Demonstrate by showing some shapes and asking the children to tell you what fraction of each shape is shaded, for example:

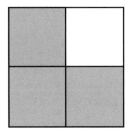 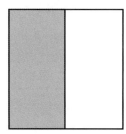 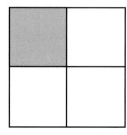 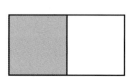

Give each pair of children some pictures of squares, rectangles, circles and triangles. Ask them to divide the shapes into halves and quarters if possible, shade one part and label.

### *Plenary*
Ask some of the children to explain what they did.
Tell the children, that now they can find halves and quarters of shapes, the next step is to identify halves and quarters of amounts.

## 12. Arrays

> **Objective:** Understand multiplication as describing an array
> **Leading to:** Recognising that multiplication can be done in any order
> **Strand:** Calculations
> **Topic:** Understanding multiplication

### *Group activity*
Drawing arrays and writing down the multiplication facts from them.

Demonstrate by putting eight counters on the OHP or eight dots on the board and arranging them into rows of equal size.

 **OR**

Give the groups 12 counters and ask them to make and label as above as many arrays as they can. Then ask them to do the same for 16, 20 and 24 counters.

*Plenary*

Invite some children to show everyone one of the arrays they made by demonstrating on the OHP and labelling on the board.

Next, tell the children that they will be using the work that they have been doing today to help them recognise that multiplication can be done in any order. Use the example you started with at the beginning of the lesson to make this clear.

Tell the children that this will be helpful if they need to work out what 3 x 6 is and they do not know their six times table. They can simply turn the numbers around and work out 6 x 3.

## 13. Division

Objective: Understand the operation of division as sharing and associated vocabulary
Leading to: Understanding the operation of division as repeated subtraction
Strand: Calculations
Topic: Understanding division

*Group activity*

Understanding division as sharing so that they can answer problems such as:
Six sweets are to be shared equally between two children. How many sweets does each child get?

Give a practical demonstration of division by sharing, by sharing equally a certain number of items between different numbers of children.
Give each group a pile of cubes, counters or something similar and ask them to find as many ways to divide their objects equally into groups as possible. Can they make up a number story to go with each example?

$12 \div 3 = 4$
12 biscuits were shared equally between Sam, Pete and Sally. How many did they each get?

$12 \div 4 = 3$
12 apples were shared equally into 4 piles.
How many were in each pile?

$12 \div 6 = 2$
12 books were shared equally between6 children.
How many did each get?

$12 \div 2 = 6$
£12 were shared equally between Carol and Adam.
How many did each get?

*Plenary*

Invite some of the children to tell the others their number stories and act them out using imaginary props.

Say to the children that now they have understood this objective, they will be looking at a different way of dividing next time. They will be dividing by grouping so that they can answer problems such as:

There are 15 apples in a box. How many bags of three apples can be filled?

Demonstrate an example practically.

## 14. One-step problems

> **Objectives:** Explain methods and reasoning; writing a number sentence to show how the one-step problem was solved
> **Leading to:** Two-step problems
> **Strand:** Solving problems
> **Topic:** 'Real life' problems

*Group activity*

Solving one-step problems using number sentences.

Begin by asking the children to imagine the following problems: "Close your eyes. Imagine two children have eight cakes each. How many are there altogether?"
"One child gives two cakes to the other. How many do they each have now?"
Each time ask the children to explain how they worked these out. Show them how to write these up as number sentences:
8 + 8 = 16 or 8 x 2 = 16, so there will be 16 altogether.
And then:
8 – 2 = 6, 8 + 2 = 10, so one will have 6 and the other 10.
Give the children some problem cards, similar to the ones below and ask them to work out number sentences for each one.

> There are 16 plums. Eight children share them equally. How many plums does each child have?

> My friend has 12 teddy bears. She was given four more. How many does she now have?

Next, ask the children to make up their own stories and write number sentences for them.

## Plenary

Invite some children to tell the rest of the class one of their own stories and see if the rest of the class can make up the number sentences that go with them.

Tell the children that, because they have worked so hard and done so well, next time they will be solving two-step problems, which are the most common type of problem they will encounter.

## Example

Story: There are two adults and four children in each of the ten families that live in our road. How many people are there altogether?
Number sentence: 2 + 4 = 6 then 6 x 10 = 60

## 15. Months and seasons

**Objectives:** Know in order the months and seasons of the year
**Leading to:** Knowing significant times in the day and year
**Strand:** Measures
**Topic:** Time

## Group activity

Ordering months of the year and matching them to the seasons

Introduce the group activity by showing cards with the months of the year written on them and asking the children to order them.

| | | |
|---|---|---|
| November | April | January |
| May | December | February |
| October | June | September |
| July | March | August |

Show some pictures of the seasons and ask the children to label and then order them.
See photocopiable sheet 17.

For group work, present the children with some more pictures and labels for the months of the year. Ask them to make posters by matching, grouping and then sticking them in order with the appropriate seasons, as shown below.

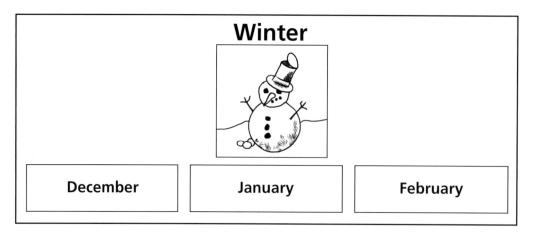

*Plenary*

Ask the groups to show their posters and explain why they made the decisions they made. Tell the children, that next time they will be thinking about special things that happen at different times of the year. Demonstrate an example: start with birthdays, give the children a name label to stick onto a month of the year chart, as shown below.

**Our Birthdays**

| January | February | March | April | May | June |
|---------|----------|-------|-------|-----|------|
| Jodie | Adam | | Caroline | Dave | |
| | Charlie | | | | |

Ask the children to think about other special times for the next lesson.

## 16. Right angles

**Objectives:** Recognise that the corners of doors, windows and so on are right angles and that a square and rectangle have right angles at each corner
**Leading to:** Making and drawing half and quarter turns and linking quarter turns to right angles
**Strand:** Shape and space
**Topic:** Movement and angle

## Group activity
Looking for right angles in the classroom and recognising right angles in shapes.

Demonstrate a right angle using your arms and thumb and forefinger. Ask the children to copy you. Give the children a piece of paper and ask them to identify the right angles. Ask them to fold their piece of paper: can they still see any right angles? Repeat this. In groups, ask the children to look around the classroom to see if they can find any right angles. Give them an example such as the classroom door. They need to draw and label (with arrows) the right angles that they can see. Give them a large piece of paper so that they can make a poster, with contributions from each member of the group as shown below.

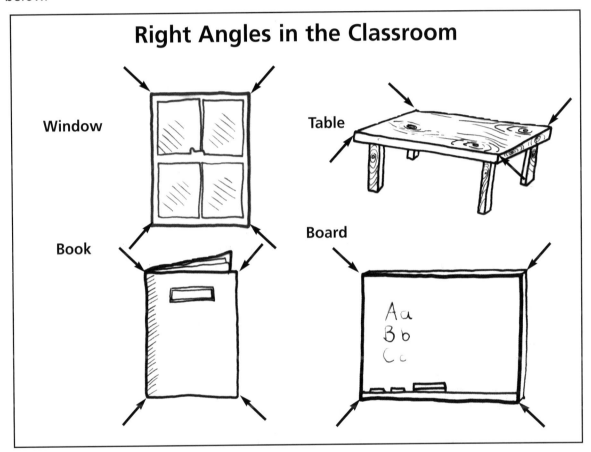

## Plenary
Invite some of the groups to show the rest of the class their posters and explain which objects they used, where the right angles are and how they know.

Show the children some squares and rectangles and ask them to tell you where the right angles are. Ask them if they think that all squares and rectangles have four right angles at the corners. Can they make this a rule for one of the properties of the two shapes?

Tell them that now they can identify right angles, during the next lesson they will be making and drawing them, using clocks and geo-strips and that they will be linking them to quarter turns (one right angle) and half turns (two right angles). Demonstrate what you mean using a clock. Ask questions such as: "If I put the hands on the 12 and 3, can you see a right angle?"; "Where else could I put the hands to make a right angle?"; "If I put both hands on the 12 and then move one round to make a right angle, I am making a quarter of a turn. If I put both hands on the 12 and then move one hand to the 3 and then on to the 6, how many right angles have I made?"; "If moving from the 12 to the 3 is a quarter turn what do you think the size of the turn is from the 12 to the 6?"

# Photocopiable Sheet 14
## Number sequences

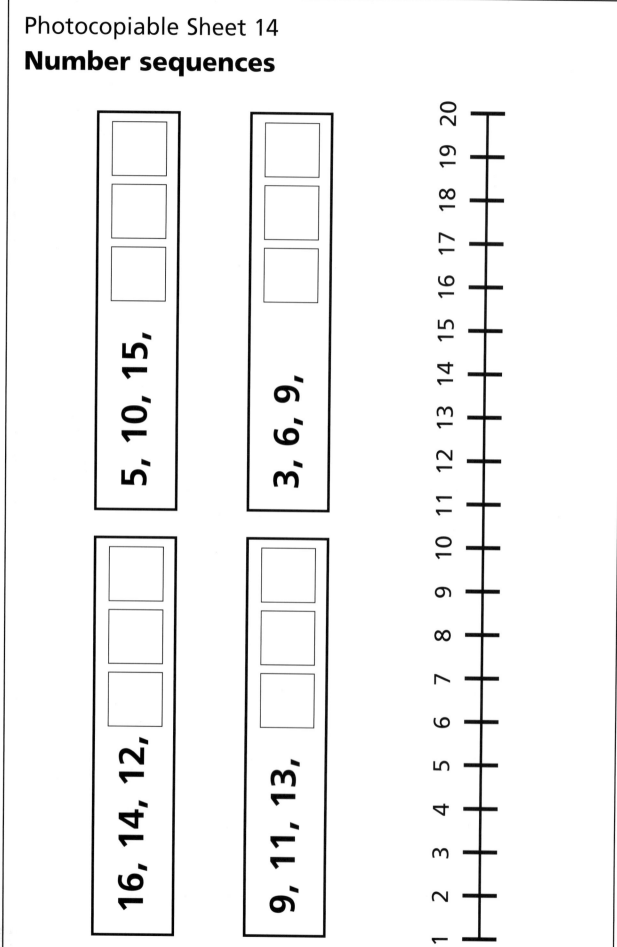

5, 10, 15,

3, 6, 9,

16, 14, 12,

9, 11, 13,

1  2  3  4  5  6  7  8  9  10  11  12  13  14  15  16  17  18  19  20

# Photocopiable Sheet 15
# **Estimating**

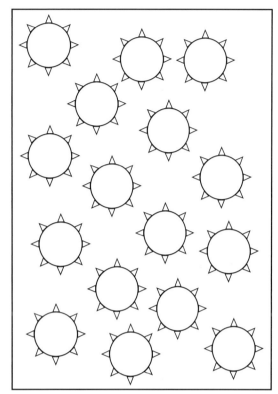

# Photocopiable Sheet 16
# **Subtraction**

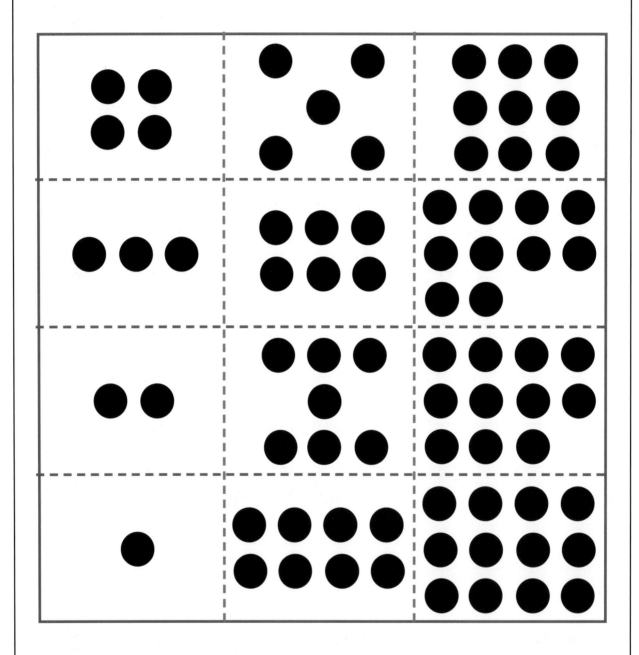

© The Questions Publishing Company Ltd

# Photocopiable Sheet 17
# Months and seasons

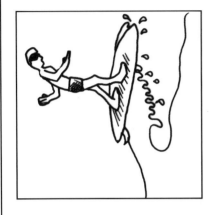

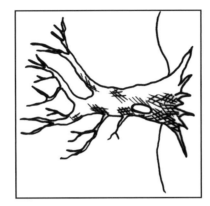

Winter

Winter

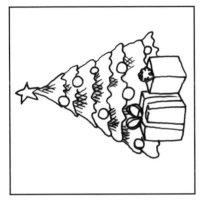

Winter

Autumn

Summer

Spring

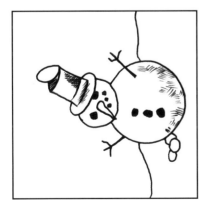

Summer

Spring

# Chapter 3
# Links to other maths topics and curriculum areas

The Framework for Teaching Mathematics has a very helpful section on making links between the subjects. It states that 'you need to look for opportunities for drawing mathematical experience out of a wide range of children's activities.'
Maths contributes to many subjects in the primary curriculum, often in practical ways, and these links often help to validate the purposes of maths.
Maths and other areas of curriculum subjects can complement each other. It is important that links are made as it helps the children to see the relevance of what they are learning in the overall picture of their education. It is often too easy to treat the curriculum subjects as isolated areas that must be covered. Linking makes it all the more real to the children as it can put what they are learning into contexts they can appreciate.

Subject links (extracts from the NNS Framework):

**English:** Maths lessons can help develop and support pupils' literacy skills by teaching mathematical vocabulary and technical terms, asking children to read and interpret problems to identify the mathematical content and by encouraging them to explain, argue and present conclusions to others.
**Science:** Almost every scientific investigation or experiment is likely to require one or more of the mathematical skills of classifying, counting, measuring, calculating, estimating and recording in tables and graphs.
**Art, D & T:** Measurements are often needed in art and design and technology. Many patterns and constructions are based on spatial ideas and properties of shapes including symmetry.
**ICT**: Children will apply and use mathematics in a variety of ways when they solve problems using ICT. For example, they will collect and classify data, enter it into data-handling software, produce graphs and tables, and interpret and explain their results.
**History, geography and RE:** In various circumstances children will collect data by counting and measuring, use co-ordinates, ideas of angle, direction, position, scale and ratio. Patterns of days of the week, the calendar, annual festivals and passages of time all have a mathematical basis.
**PE and music:** These often require measurement of height, distance and time, counting, symmetry, movement, position and direction.

Plenary sessions can be used to discuss work carried out in the objectives taught and linked to work that has been or will be studied in subjects such those mentioned.

This chapter is designed to show where some of the possible links are, in order to get you thinking about making links in literacy, science, history, geography, art, and PE as well as other maths topics.

# Literacy

Links between numeracy and literacy are plentiful.

In the Curriculum Guidelines for English, it states that children should be taught to:

✪ Speak clearly, fluently and confidently to different people;
✪ Listen, understand and respond to others;
✪ Join as members of a group;
✪ Participate in a range of drama activities;
✪ Be part of group discussion and interaction;
✪ Be introduced to some of the main features of spoken standard English and taught to use them.

In maths all of these are encouraged as a matter of course by, for example:

✪ Explaining strategies to others;
✪ Listening to and discussing other children's methods of working out calculations;
✪ Working on activities in a group;
✪ Imagining and acting out problems in the problem solving strand;
✪ Discussing and interacting with each other in group work;
✪ Learning, understanding and using new vocabulary.

# Year 1

### 1. Counting

> **Objective:** Know the number names and recite them in order, from and back to zero
> **Strand:** Numbers and the number system
> **Topic:** Counting, properties of numbers and number sequences

### *Plenary*

During the plenary revise the counting that the class has been working on (Lesson 2 in Chapter 1). Sing some number rhymes such as 'One, two, three, four, five; once I caught a fish alive'; 'Ten Green Bottles'; 'Ten Fat Sausages'.
Then tell the children that during their next literacy lesson, they will be listening to the story of 'The Hungry Caterpillar'(and that the work they have been doing today will help them with the counting they need to do during the story. Have a quick look at the book, so that the children will recognise it when they see it next time).

## 2. Ordering ordinal numbers

> **Objective:** Understand and use the vocabulary of comparing and ordering numbers, including ordinal numbers
> **Strand:** Numbers and the number system
> **Topic:** Place value and ordering

### *Plenary*

During the plenary revise the ordinal numbers you have been working with (Lesson 3 in Chapter 1).

Tell the children that this work will help them in their next literacy lesson when they will be looking at the story of 'The Jolly Postman'(by Janet and Allan Ahlberg) and all the houses he has to visit. Briefly show the children the book. Another story that is a helpful link is 'The Hare and the Tortoise'.

## 3. Number lines

> **Objective:** Order a set of familiar numbers and position them on a number line
> **Strand:** Numbers and the number system
> **Topic:** Place value and ordering

### *Possible activities*

Shuffle the cards from 1 to 20 and ask the children to order them.

Display the numbers from 1 to 10, swap two over. Can the children identify which two have been changed?

Put in order sets of objects.

Pick between four to six random numbers from 1 to 20 and put in order smallest first.

As above but put in order with largest first.

Use a blank 1 to 20 number line and ask the children to place number cards in the correct order on the line.

### *Plenary*

Use a number line from 1 to 26. Display a coding chart, linking letters of the alphabet with the numbers 1 to 26. See photocopiable sheet 18.

Ask the children to find the number that matches the first letter of their name. Once they have, they need to write that letter and put it on the number line in the correct place, for example Tom will look at the chart, find T and the number 20, write T and stick it on the number 20 using Blutac. Discuss where the different letters are, how many numbers there are between certain letters, which letter matches with the highest number.

Tell them that this will help them during their literacy lesson when they will be looking at the initial letter of their name and putting the names in the class in alphabetical order.

## 4. Story problems

### Possible activities
Is there enough information to solve the problem or too much? [Bold]

### Examples
"Sam had 10p. Did he have enough money to buy the sweets?"
*There is not enough information.*
"Chris spent 5p on a lolly. How much change did she get?"
*Again, there is not enough information.*
"Imran had a lovely dog, she was black with some white spots and loved eating bacon. She had three puppies. How many dogs did he have altogether?"
*There is too much information.*

## 5. Visualising problems

### Examples
After singing 'Ten fat sausages', ask the children to close their eyes and imagine those sausages sizzling away. Now ask them to imagine four popping and banging and jumping out of the pan. How many are left sizzling?

After singing '1, 2, 3, 4, 5, Once I caught a fish alive', ask the children to imagine catching the fish and putting it in a bucket of water. Ask the children to describe their fish. Now ask them to imagine that they have caught three more fish exactly the same and put them in the bucket. How many are in the bucket now?

Ask the children to close their eyes and imagine a tree. Tell them it is short and round with green leaves. Can they see it? On the tree there are five red apples. Tell the children to put the apples on their tree. Can they see them? They look really tasty. Explain that the children want to eat one so they take one of those apples off the tree. How many are left on the tree?
Tell them to take two more off. How many are on the tree now?

After singing 'Ten green bottles hanging on the wall', ask the children to imagine an empty shelf with no green bottles. Ask the children to put two bottles on the shelf, now another three. How many are on the shelf now?

## 6. Acting out problems

### *Example*
Sam, Adam, Jenny, Peter and Jane are having a picnic. Peter has brought 20 biscuits to share equally with Jane. How many will they each have?

The group needs to have five children in it. The children should first prepare 20 paper cut-out biscuits. They could begin their mime by sitting down and pretending to eat. The child who is playing Peter could share out the circles between the others. Then each child could stand up in turn and show how many biscuits they have.

The children will probably come up with some great ideas of their own! See lesson idea 5 in Chapter 1.

### *Plenary*
During the plenary ask one or two of the groups to act out their scene and ask the rest of the class what they think it is all about and the possible answer.
Link this to literacy by telling them that during their next numeracy lesson they will be acting out some of their own scenes to fit in with situations that you will give them.
(NC ref: participating in a range of drama activities). It could be effective to link the ideas from the numeracy lesson.

# Year 2

## 1. Ordering numbers

> **Objective:** Understand and use the vocabulary of comparing and ordering numbers, including ordinal numbers
> **Strand:** Numbers and the number system
> **Topic:** Place value and ordering

Teach the children the rhyme for the numbers of days in the months: 'Thirty days has September, April, June and November, All the rest have 31, except for February which has 28'.
Match up the months with numbers showing how many days they have.
See photocopiable sheets 19 and 20.
Order the days in each month, writing them correctly: 1st, 2nd, 3rd, 4th, and so on.
Using a number square ask the children to put a marker on the number signifying how many days there are in certain months. Work out how many months have 30 days, 31 days and 28/29 days.
Put markers on a number square to show the date of the children's birthdays.
Ask questions such as 'Which is the 5th month?'
Ask the children to write today's date.

### *Plenary*
Discuss the work completed during the lesson and tell the children that this will help them during literacy when they have to write the proper date in their books.

## 2. Mental calculations

**Objective:** Use knowledge that addition can be done in any order
**Strand:** Calculations
**Topic:** Mental calculation strategies (+ and -)

### *Plenary*

After a lesson on adding numbers mentally by looking for pairs of numbers that make 10 and adding these first or starting with the largest number first, display a chart linking the letters of the alphabet and corresponding numbers. See photocopiable sheet 18.
Ask the children to work out the value of their first name. Explain that they need to use their knowledge of the alphabet and spelling, studied in literacy, as well as what they have learnt today to help them.

## 3. 2-D and 3-D shapes

**Objective:** Describe and classify common 3-D or 2-D shapes according to their properties
**Strand:** Shape and space
**Topic:** Properties of 3-D and 2-D shapes

### *Possible activities*

Collect examples of cubes, cuboids, cylinders, spheres and pyramids and match them to name labels.
As above for circles, triangles, rectangles, squares, pentagons, hexagons and octagons.
Sort the shapes according to different criteria for example, triangular or rectangular faces, less than four sides or more than five sides.
Describe a shape to a friend for them to identify.

### *Plenary*

Revise the vocabulary of properties of shape and their names.
Tell the children that in their literacy lesson they will need to remember the names of the shapes as they will be using them to make alliterations, for example:
'Colourful cubes can't count.'
'Soft squares smell sausagey.'

## 4. Word problems

**Objective:** Solve simple word problems set in 'real life' contexts and explain how the problem was solved
**Strand:** Solving Problems
**Topic:** 'Real life' problems

### *Possible activities*
**Which operation should we use?**

## Examples

Katie bought four comics, each costing 10p. How much did she spend?
Multiply or add – discuss which would be the most efficient method.

Flowers are put in bunches of ten. Tess has 34 flowers. How many bunches can she make and how many flowers will be left over?
Divide – discuss how you would find the remainder.

Rob bought a comic for 45p and a notebook for £1.20. How much did he spend?
Add.

**Use visualising problems**

## Examples

Ben has three goldfish. They love to swim around in their bowl. Imagine the goldfish in their bowl. Can you see them? They blow big bubbles. Each fish blows two bubbles. How many bubbles are there?

If each fish blows two bubbles and there are ten bubbles, how many fish are there? Close your eyes and imagine ten bubbles, two for each fish. How many fish do you need for all the bubbles?

Close your eyes, imagine that you are at the seaside. Describe where you are. At the seaside there is a rock pool. Have a look in the rock pool, what can you see inside it? I can see five crabs in mine. Imagine there are five crabs in yours. Go to another rock pool, this time you can see three crabs. What is the difference between the number of crabs in each pool? How many crabs are there altogether in both rock pools?

## Plenary

Discuss the work of the lesson.
Give groups a scenario to do with a 'real life' problem and ask them to read it and discuss amongst themselves what they might do. Tell them that during the next literacy lesson they will be using these to make up short plays (to convey situations, characters and emotions).

## Examples

"My dad drove us all to the seaside. We got stuck in a traffic jam. It took five hours and a half hour to get there. We left at 9am. What time did we arrive?"
Emotions to convey: annoyance and boredom.

"Mr Smith has grown six tomato plants. On each plant there are six tomatoes. He was so pleased that he went out and told all his friends. How many tomatoes has he grown altogether?"
Emotions to convey: happiness and pleasure.

"Jenny baked 22 biscuits. She shared them between herself and her two friends. She gave the left-overs to her brother. Why wasn't he happy?"
Emotions to convey: sadness and anger.

# Science

Links between numeracy and science are plentiful. They mostly come under the strand of Handling data, although working with numbers and measures obviously plays an important part.

In the Curriculum Guidelines for Science, it states that children should be taught to:

✪ Ask questions, e.g. 'How?', 'Why?', 'What will happen if…?' and decide how they might find answers to them.
✪ Think about what might happen before deciding what to do.
✪ Explore, using the senses of sight, hearing, smell, touch and taste as appropriate, and make and record observations and measurements.
✪ Communicate what happened in a variety of ways for example, by drawings, tables, block graphs and pictograms.
✪ Make simple comparisons, for example hand span, shoe size.
✪ Review their work and explain what they did to others.

In maths all of these are encouraged in different ways, for example:

✪ Asking questions such as; "Which is the best way to answer this calculation?", "What would happen if I did it this way?", "What do I need to know to solve this problem?";
✪ Estimating answers;
✪ Recording measurements with length, mass, capacity and time;
✪ Solving a problem by collecting, representing and interpreting data;
✪ Making comparisons in number, shapes and measures;
✪ Checking and explaining strategies.

The Handling data strand is probably the best way to link the two subjects. There are five aspects of data handling in numeracy that need to be considered:

✪ Specifying the problem – formulating questions in terms of the data that is needed and the type of inferences that can be made from them.
✪ Planning – decide what data needs collecting, including sample size and data format and what statistical analysis needs to be carried out.
✪ Collecting data – from a variety of appropriate sources including experiments, surveys and primary and secondary data.
✪ Processing and representing – including lists, tables and charts.
✪ Interpreting and discussion – relate the summarised data to the initial question.

It is often appropriate to use a problem that needs solving in science to satisfy these requirements. The interpreting and discussion aspect can be achieved during the plenary session and then taken into the science lesson to use as needed.
This part of the chapter concentrates on possible problems that can be solved in numeracy and then taken into the science lesson.
A good format for a lesson on Handling data can be found in Chapter 2, Year 1, lesson idea 8. This can be adapted to suit most situations.

# Years 1 and 2

## 1. Growing plants

> **Objective:** to recognise that there are different plants in the immediate environment
> **Numeracy:** Handling data lesson

### Problem
In the science lesson, the children will be finding out about the different plants around school, so will need to know what they are. During this lesson they will be finding out this information and taking it to the next science session.

### Collection
Find some examples, identifying them if possible.

### Representation
Show the information in a chart form, indicating whether the plants are common or not.

### Plenary
Discuss the information obtained and tell the children that during science they will be focusing on two of their found plants to find out where they grow and how to take care of them.

## 2. Sorting and using materials A

> **Objective:** to recognise that every material has many properties which can be recognised using our senses and described using appropriate vocabulary
> **Numeracy:** Handling data lesson

### Problem
In the science lesson the children will be looking at the properties of materials, and so need to be able to sort them using their senses. This is the purpose of this lesson.

### Collection
Provide a selection of materials from those you intend to use in science.

### Representation
Sort the materials practically into groups that can be recognised by smell, touch or hearing. Some items may need to be put in more than one set.

### Plenary
Make a list of the findings. You scribe and the children tell you which items belong in which group.
Tell the children that they will be using this information in their next science lesson to help with the rest of their investigation into the properties of materials.

### 3. Sorting and using materials B

> **Objective:** to recognise that everyday objects can be made from the same material
> **Numeracy:** Handling data lesson

#### *Problem*
What materials are particular objects in the classroom made from?

#### *Collection*
Choose some materials such as plastic, metal, wood. Ask the children to look for some classroom objects made from these. Make up a collection.

#### *Representation*
Make up a block graph to show how many items are made from each of the materials.

#### *Plenary*
Ask the children what the graph shows, expect lots of comments. Ask which is the most common material, how many things are made from it and so on.
Tell the children that they will be looking further at the graph during science to find out why certain materials are good for making lots of different items.

### 4. Health and growth

> **Objective:** to know that we eat different kinds of food, to collect information and to present results as a block graph
> **Numeracy:** Handling data lesson

#### *Problem*
During science the children will be learning about different foods that we eat. Start by finding out the answer to this question: 'What are our favourite foods?'

#### *Collection*
Ask the children to choose their favourite food, make a tally.

#### *Representation*
Make up a block graph using the 'post it' note idea from Chapter 2 (Page 35)

#### *Plenary*
Discuss the graph by asking questions and asking the children to ask you questions about what it shows.
Find out what conclusions can be made from it.
Tell the children that this will be very useful information for the science lesson.
Repeat this activity for the following science objectives:

- ✪ to know that we need exercise to stay healthy
- ✪ to make and record observations
- ✪ to make simple comparisons

#### *Another problem to solve in Numeracy and then take into Science*
What type of exercise do we take regularly?

# History

Links between numeracy and history are evident in the strands of Calculations and Solving Problems.

In the Curriculum Guidelines for History, it states that children should be taught to:

✪ Place events and objects in chronological order.

In maths, this Attainment Target can be supported during the teaching of different topics, for example:

✪ Number operations and the relationship between them;
✪ Developing rapid recall of number facts;
✪ Developing a range of mental strategies for finding, from known facts, those that they cannot recall;
✪ Carrying out simple calculations;
✪ Choosing sensible calculation methods to solve whole-number problems.

# Years 1 and 2

### 1. Unit 2 (Year 1) What were homes like a long time ago?
How were homes long ago different from homes today?
Identify the key features of a home built a long time ago.
Identify differences between two homes built at different times.

### *Plenary*
During the plenary session of numeracy lessons to do with ordering numbers or using a number line, select some pictures of homes from long ago which you will be using during your history topic on homes. Ask the children to order them on a blank number line and add the ordinal numbers – the earliest being 1st.
Do the same thing with the numbers of the actual dates or centuries.
It is best to use this idea when you are actually working on this topic and do not forget to tell the children why.

### 2. Unit 3 (Year 1/2) What were seaside holidays like in the past?
This unit compares seaside holidays in the recent past with those taken a long time ago. Children will develop an understanding of chronology.

### *Plenary*
Again, use number lines during the plenary session, particularly with ordinal numbers. Have a collection of holiday photos. Tell the children that as this is part of their history topic they will be ordering them from past to present. Ask the children to put them where they think they go on a blank number line, ordering them from earliest (1st) to latest.

### 3. Unit 4 (Year 2) Why do we remember Florence Nightingale?
This unit looks at the life of Florence Nightingale, why she went to the Crimea, and what happened as a result of her work.

*Plenary*
Another number line activity similar to the others, linked in the same way to the history topic and to the objectives of the numeracy lesson. This time include working out the number of years between the important parts of Florence Nightingale's life and those of the children. Employ in this various calculation strategies involved in addition and subtraction.

# Geography

Links between numeracy and geography are obvious when looking at the strand Shape and space within the topics of Position and direction and Movement and angle. Various aspects can be incorporated into Handling data.
In the Curriculum Guidelines for Geography, it states that children should be taught to:

✪ Observe and record, for example identify buildings in the street and complete a chart;
✪ Communicate in different ways;
✪ Use geographical vocabulary such as 'river', 'motorway', 'near', 'far', 'north', 'south';
✪ Use globes, maps and plans at a range of scales, for example following a route on a map;
✪ Make maps and plans, for example a pictorial map of a place in a story.

In maths all of these are encouraged in different ways, for example:

✪ Solve a relevant problem by using simple lists, tables and charts to sort, classify and organise information;
✪ Use the correct language, symbols and vocabulary associated with number and data;
✪ Communicate in spoken, pictorial and written form, at first using informal language and recording, then mathematical language and symbols;
✪ Present results in an organised way;
✪ Observe, visualise and describe positions, directions and movements using common words;
✪ Recognise movements in a straight line (translations) and rotations, and combine them in simple ways for example, give instructions to get to a nearby place such as the school library.

# Years 1 and 2

### 1. Unit 1 (Year 1): Around our school – the local area
This is a 'long' unit. It uses investigative tasks to introduce children to the idea of looking at their local area.
The local area will be studied frequently during a child's time in primary school and therefore this unit focuses on aspects of local features, land use and environment.

### Possible numeracy lesson ideas
Talk about a journey for example, how to go home from school, how to follow a track painted on the playground.
Follow instructions for a short journey for example, how to get to the library.
For each of the above make sure you use the appropriate vocabulary.
Devise instructions to make a floor robot reach a particular place.

*Plenary*
Tell the children that the work they have been doing in numeracy will help them in their geography topic about their local area. Ask the children to close their eyes and imagine the journey you are going to tell them. Give instructions to a place in the school such as the hall, Year 4 classroom, staffroom.
Don't tell them where they are going.
Ask where they are at the end.

## 2. Unit 5 (Year 1/2): Where in the world is Barnaby Bear?
This is a 'continuous' unit, designed to be developed at various points throughout the key stage. It uses a first-hand object – Barnaby the teddy bear – to enable children to learn about other countries and places. Barnaby travels with different people connected to the school as well as on school visits, creating a sense of personal involvement for the children.

*Possible numeracy lesson ideas*
Devise a simple scale (as the crow flies), to follow Barnaby's journey.
Use a bear and call him Barnaby and take him on a journey around the classroom using straight movements and quarter and half clockwise or anticlockwise turns.
Give instructions for Barnaby to follow to find a route through a simple maze drawn on squared paper.
Describe the position of a picture of Barnaby on a simple map in different ways.

*Plenary*
Link the work that they have been doing in their geography topic. Give a volunteer a teddy bear, blindfold them and ask some of the children to help guide them to a pretend jar of honey. The children must use the appropriate language.

# Art

Links between numeracy and art are evident in the strand of Shape and space.
In the Curriculum Guidelines for Art, it states that children should be taught about:

✪ Visual and tactile elements, including colour, pattern and texture, line and tone, shape, form and space;
✪ Working on their own, and collaborating with others, on projects in two and three dimensions and on different scales.

In maths, these Attainment Targets can be supported during the teaching of different topics, for example:

✪ Describing properties of shapes that they can see or visualise using the related vocabulary;
✪ Creating 2-D shapes and 3-D shapes;
✪ Recognising reflective symmetry in familiar 2-D shapes and patterns.

# Years 1 and 2

## 1. Unit 2B (Year 1/2): Mother Nature, designer
In this unit, children explore line, shape, colour and texture in natural forms. They make observations of natural objects and use their observations as the basis for textile design. They use their experience of fabrics to make a collage and learn and use simple techniques for appliqué.

## 2. Unit 1C (Year 1/2): What is sculpture?

In this unit, children develop their understanding of shape, form, texture and the sensory qualities of materials. They learn about the work of sculptors and about different kinds of sculpture, including those made of natural materials. They also learn skills for arranging materials they have collected to make a relief collage and a sculpture.

### Possible numeracy lesson ideas

Talk about shapes and patterns in leaves.
Talk about the shapes in curtains, clothes, materials.
Design their own patterns using the 2-D shapes relevant to their year group.
Make halves of paper shapes by folding and make them into symmetrical patterns.
Combine four squares to make new shapes.
Use pin boards and elastic bands to make irregular pentagons and hexagons.
Make, talk about and describe symmetrical patterns made by ink blots or paint.

### Plenary sessions

At the beginning of each plenary tell the children of the links you are making with their artwork. Show suitable pictures or artefacts to illustrate what these links are. Look at the children's work and compare to the artwork that is relevant. Tell the children what they will be doing in art as a result of their numeracy work.

# PE

Links between numeracy and PE are evident in the strand of Shape and space, and the topics Position and direction, and Movement and angle.

In the Curriculum Guidelines for PE, it states that children should be taught to:

✪ Use movement imaginatively, responding to stimuli, including music, and performing basic skills for example, travelling, being still, making a shape, jumping, turning and gesturing;
✪ Change the rhythm, speed, level and direction of their movements.

In the Framework for teaching Mathematics, it is suggested that work covered in the following parts of the numeracy lesson can be reinforced during PE:

✪ Follow and give instructions to move in particular directions: climb upwards, downwards, towards, away from, across, along, through, turn to the left or right, move forwards, backwards or sideways;
✪ Move clockwise, anti-clockwise, face inwards, face outwards.

During plenary sessions make reference to the fact that you will be following up certain activities physically in PE.

# Other areas of maths

During plenary sessions for work on numbers and the number system, make links to measures and money. For example, ask questions such as:

✪ 1 have 10p, Sue has 20p and Pete has 30p. How much do we have altogether?

✪ My friends and I were tying up parcels. John had a length of string that was double the length of mine. Mine was 50cms long. How long was John's? Sam's was half as long as mine. How long was Sam's?

✪ My kitten weighed 5kg. My friend's cat was twice as heavy. How heavy was her cat?

Including aspects of data handling during plenaries related to other areas is a useful way of reinforcing work done previously in this topic. It provides a useful link and promotes the relevance of data handling in general.

Draw some tables or charts on the board and put information onto them that is relevant to the objective you have been teaching, for example:

> **Objective:** Read the time to the hour or half hour on analogue clocks

| Our bedtimes | | | | | | | | | |
|---|---|---|---|---|---|---|---|---|---|
| 7 o'clock | ☺ | ☺ | ☺ | ☺ | ☺ | ☺ | ☺ | | |
| half past 7 | ☺ | ☺ | ☺ | ☺ | ☺ | ☺ | ☺ | ☺ | ☺ |
| 8 o'clock | ☺ | ☺ | ☺ | ☺ | ☺ | | | | |

Ask questions such as:

✪ How many children go to bed at half past 7?

✪ How many children are in bed by half past 7?

✪ How many children are still up after 7 o'clock?

✪ How many children go to bed at 8 o'clock?

**Objective:** Use and begin to read the vocabulary related to mass

These children went shopping and bought some fruit.

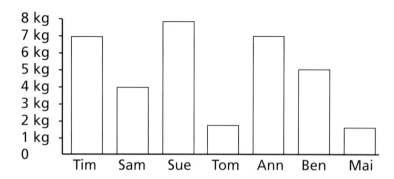

Ask questions such as:

✪ Who bought the most fruit?

✪ How much did Ben and Mai buy together?

✪ What is the difference in weight between Sue's fruit and Sam's fruit?

✪ Who bought 7 kg of fruit?

**Objective:** Find totals of amounts of money and give change

This table shows the amounts of money some children spent.

| Sally | £1.25 |
|-------|-------|
| Aaron | £3.00 |
| Ahmed | £2.75 |
| Won   | 50p   |
| Chris | 75p   |
| Peter | £2.50 |

Ask questions such as:

✪ Who spent the most?

✪ How much did Won and Peter spend altogether?

✪ If the book Ahmed wanted to buy cost £3. How much more money would he need?

✪ If Aaron gave the shopkeeper £5, how much change would he receive?
   What about Sally? Peter?

✪ Which two children spent £4 altogether?

| Objective: | Recognise odd and even numbers |
|---|---|

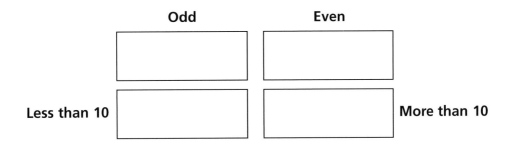

Hold up some single and two-digit numbers (with Blutak on the back). Ask children to come to the front to sort them in to the correct boxes.

You could sort using this type of diagram (which appeared in the 2001 SAT's test)

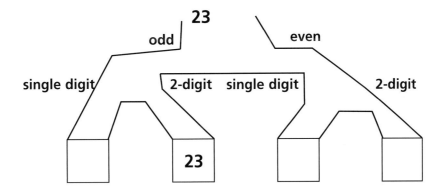

Put the work you have been doing into a real-life problem context by visualising, asking the children to make up a problem, or challenging them with a problem you have devised. This will be covered more thoroughly in the next chapter.

These three methods will reinforce the relevance of the maths that they have learning.

## Photocopiable Sheet 18

## Code chart

| A | B | C | D | E | F | G | H | I | J |
|---|---|---|---|---|---|---|---|---|---|
| 1 | 2 | 3 | 4 | 5 | 6 | 7 | 8 | 9 | 10 |

| K | L | M | N | O | P | Q | R | S | T |
|---|---|---|---|---|---|---|---|---|---|
| 11 | 12 | 13 | 14 | 15 | 16 | 17 | 18 | 19 | 20 |

| U | V | W | X | Y | Z |
|---|---|---|---|---|---|
| 21 | 22 | 23 | 24 | 25 | 26 |

# Photocopiable Sheet 19
## Days of the month A

**January**

**February**

**March**

**April**

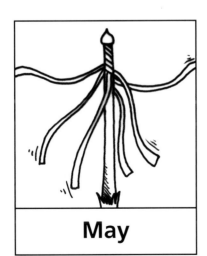

**May**

**June**

# Days of the month B

**July**

**August**

**September**

**October**

**November**

**December**

| 28 | 30 | 31 |

# Chapter 4
# Problem solving and games

Using and applying the skills that the children have been taught is one of the most important elements of numeracy. Ideas need to be put into context for the children so they can see the sense and relevance of what they have learnt. Many children have difficulty with problem-solving activities so it is vital to provide them with lots of short sessions in which to practise these skills. The plenary part of the lesson can help, as it is an opportunity to put what they have been learning into a 'real life' situation.

After lessons from the strands of Numbers and the number system, Calculations, Addition, Subtraction and Mental calculation strategies, incorporate some of the ideas below within your plenaries to help put the more abstract number work into context.

## Visualising

Children often find visualising difficult and need to practise this skill. If they can see a word problem in their minds it will be easier for them to relate to it and therefore understand it and come up with a solution. It is also a useful way of introducing the vocabulary associated with problem solving, such as: How many more? How many altogether? What is the difference? Ask the children to close their eyes and listen carefully to what you are saying.

1. Imagine a fluffy cat. It's a girl. She's white. Imagine you are stroking her. She has some little white kittens. Three of them are playing with a ball of string. Can you see them? The other two are curled up beside their mother fast asleep. Can you see them? How many kittens has she got altogether?

2. Imagine five kittens are playing with the ball of string. Three of them run off. How many are left?

3. Imagine you are holding a frying pan. It has a sausage in it. You are frying the sausage. Now you are putting it on a plate. Now you are frying another one and putting it on the plate. Now do the same with two more. How many sausages are on your plate now? You are going to eat one, and another one and another one. How many are left?

4. Imagine you have fried three sausages and put them on the plate. Now you are going to fry three more. How many have you fried altogether?

5. Imagine Fran. What does she look like? (Ask some children to describe her).
   Poor Fran has got the measles. She has one spot on her chin, one on each leg, one on each arm and one on her tummy. Can you see them?
   How many spots does she have?
   The next morning Fran woke up with even more spots. Now she has four on her chin, two on each leg, two on each arm and four on her tummy. Can you see them?
   How many spots does she have now?

6. Imagine a leopard. What does your leopard look like? (Ask some of the children to describe their leopards, making sure they talk about the number of legs it has). All leopards have spots. This one has two spots on its tail, two spots on each of its legs, two spots on its head and two spots on its body. Can you see them?
   How many spots does it have altogether?

7. Imagine ten monkeys. Can you tell us what the monkeys look like? (Ask some children to describe their monkeys). Imagine that they are all swinging in a tree. Half of them fall off. How many are still swinging?

# Acting out

Acting out problems is a fun way of thinking about the skills needed to solve them. It helps the children think about the information that they are being given and how to use it to work through the problem. Give groups of children a short problem, some time to work out their scene and any necessary equipment such as paper, pens, coins, books, Unifix cubes, plasticine or anything which will help them.
Then ask them to mime their problem, using any pictures and props that they want to use. The rest of the class need to work out what the scene is all about and what the problem and its solution are.

### Examples
1. Pedro and Alice have been given eight sweets. Alice shares them out equally. How many will they have each?

2. Bob, Sue and Frankie went to the library. They each took out three books. How many books did they take out altogether?

3. There are twenty shoes in the cloakroom. How many children?

4. My mum shared £1 equally between my brother and me. How much were we each given?

5. Mick bought six packs of stickers. In each pack there were ten stickers. How many stickers did he have altogether?

6. Sammy and her four friends baked some cakes for the school fête. They each made ten. How many cakes did they make altogether?

7. The two cows in the field each ate 24 dandelions. How many did they eat altogether?

8. The farmer had 24 pigs and 18 horses. How many more pigs did he have than horses?

# Making up

Asking the children to make up a variety of problems from numbers or facts is a helpful way of encouraging them to think about relevant information, which operations to use and how to solve two-step problems. It enables them to put problems into a context that is meaningful to them and therefore easier for them to understand.

## *Examples*

1.         **16 cherries**          **14 plums**

My mum bought 16 cherries and 14 plums.
*How much fruit did she buy altogether?*
Our teacher brought to school 16 cherries and 14 plums.
*How many more cherries did she bring than plums?*

2.         **10 tadpoles**          **two frogs**

Two frogs each had the same number of tadpoles. There were 10 tadpoles.
*How many did each frog have?*
There were 10 tadpoles and two frogs in the pond.
*How many amphibians altogether?*

3.         **£3.50**          **£2.50**

My brother saved £3.50. My sister saved £2.50.
*How much more did my brother save?*
Sarah went to the market. She bought some flowers costing £3.50 and some fruit costing £2.50.
*How much did she spend?*

4.         **half past nine**          **1½ hours**

My family and I went to visit some friends at the seaside. We set off at half past nine. It took us 1½ hours to get there.
*At what time did we arrive?*
Peter was still doing his homework. It was half past nine. He had spent 1½ hours on it.
*At what time did he start?*

5.      **5**     **9**     **8**     **9**

We went to the zoo and saw five monkeys, nine penguins, eight giraffes and nine camels.
*How many animals did we see altogether?*
We went to the circus and saw five horses, nine clowns, eight acrobats and nine trapeze artists.
*How many more clowns were there than acrobats?*

6.      **50 cms**          **1 metre**

Katie was growing a sunflower. When she first measured it, it was 50 cms tall.
Next time she measured it, it was two metres taller.
*How tall was it?*

I made a really long worm out of plasticine. It was 50 cms long. I then stretched it until it measured one metre.
*How much longer had I made my worm?*

7.      $\frac{1}{2}$          **20**

A jumper cost £20. In the sale it was half price.
*How much did it cost in the sale?*
My friend and I had 20m of string each. I cut half of my piece off to wrap a present.
*How much more did my friend now have?*

8.      **16**          **4**

I had 16 chewy bars. I shared them between Sue, Ben, Tom and myself.
*How many did we each have?*
There were 16 monkeys. They each ate four bananas.
*How many bananas did they eat altogether?*

# Two-step problems

When using these type of problems in the plenary session, remind the children to think about:

✪ What is the important information?
✪ What do we need to find out?
✪ How will we find it out? (strategies)
✪ What will we use to help solve the problem? (pencil and paper, draw diagrams)
✪ What would be a sensible estimate?
✪ After solving it, does the answer seem sensible?

## Examples

1. There were 100 pears on the pear tree. My friend picked 30 and I picked 29. How many were left on the tree?

2. There were 100 people queuing to have a go on the roller-coaster at the theme park. Soon another 50 people joined them. Eventually 25 gave up queuing and left. How many were left in the queue?

3. Dave had collected 17 conkers; his friend gave him 12 more. He decided to save 18 and play with the others. How many did he play with?

4. Kerry had 24 books. She was given seven more for her birthday and another 13 for Christmas. How many books has she now?

5. Tim bought four oranges costing 30p each. How much change did he get from £2?

6. Theresa went to the shop and bought a loaf of bread for 75p and some milk for 45p. She gave the shopkeeper a £5 note. How much change did she receive?

7. My friend and I had one metre of ribbon each. I cut half of my piece off to wrap up a present, my friend cut a quarter of hers off and gave it to her mum. How much more than my friend did I have now?

8. At 5:00 Sam started to read a book. He read for two hours, then he watched television for 45 minutes. After that he got ready for bed. At what time did he get ready for bed?

# Playing games

Here are three simple games that you may find useful for the occasional plenary session. They can be adapted to use for any topic.

### The Grid Game or Bingo

The idea of this game is for the children to fill in their own grids (of any size but usually 3 x 3 or 3 x 2) with numbers or shapes or whatever is relevant to the lesson. You then call out types of numbers or properties of shapes. If they have any that are applicable to what you have said, they cross it out. The winner is the first player to cross out all their numbers, for example: Children fill their grid with numbers from 1 to 20. Give clues such as:

✪ the number two more than four,
✪ one of your odd numbers.

If the children have the answer on their grid they cross it out.

Other ideas could be:
a) Numbers from 10 to 100: ask vocabulary-based statements – multiples of ten, five and two, even numbers and odd numbers.
b) Any two-digit numbers: children cross out any number they have written that has the digit that you call out in the position you call it, for example if they have written 56 and you say five in the tens or 50, they cross that out.
c) Any 2-D shapes (drawn): make statements to do with their properties, for example cross out all the shapes that have four sides, any that have three corners.

### Ladders and Snakes or In the Bin
This game can also fit in with virtually any topic you might be studying. You will need a selection of around 20 cards with suitable numbers on, such as:

Numbers from 1 to 20: write these numbers on the cards, or use the number cards at the back of the book. Pick the cards randomly and, as each one is drawn, call it out; the children need to write it in a rectangle of the ladder. The aim is to fill up the ladder with numbers ordered from lowest at the bottom to highest at the top. Any that won't fit go into the snake. You can use photocopiable sheet 21. For example:
Numbers 1 to 20:
5 picked, put on 3rd section.
7 and 12 picked, put on ladder.
10 picked, but there is no space for it to fit on the ladder so it goes in the snake.

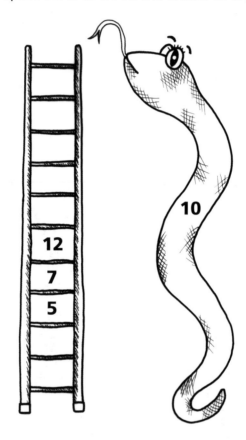

### Follow me cards, loop cards or dominoes
These three types of games are basically the same. They can be used as dominoes during a group activity or follow me cards during a plenary. During the plenary, it is often fun to finish the session with a game. You can either give a few cards to a group of two or three children or give one card to children who are confident enough to 'go solo'. One child or group calls out the question on their card. Whoever has the answer calls it out and then asks the question written on their card.
Again you can make sets for any type of topic work. Photocopiable sheets 22 and 23 show an example for rapid recall of number facts. This is a very effective way of rehearsing doubles, halves and multiplication facts.

## Photocopiable Sheet 21
# Ladders and snakes

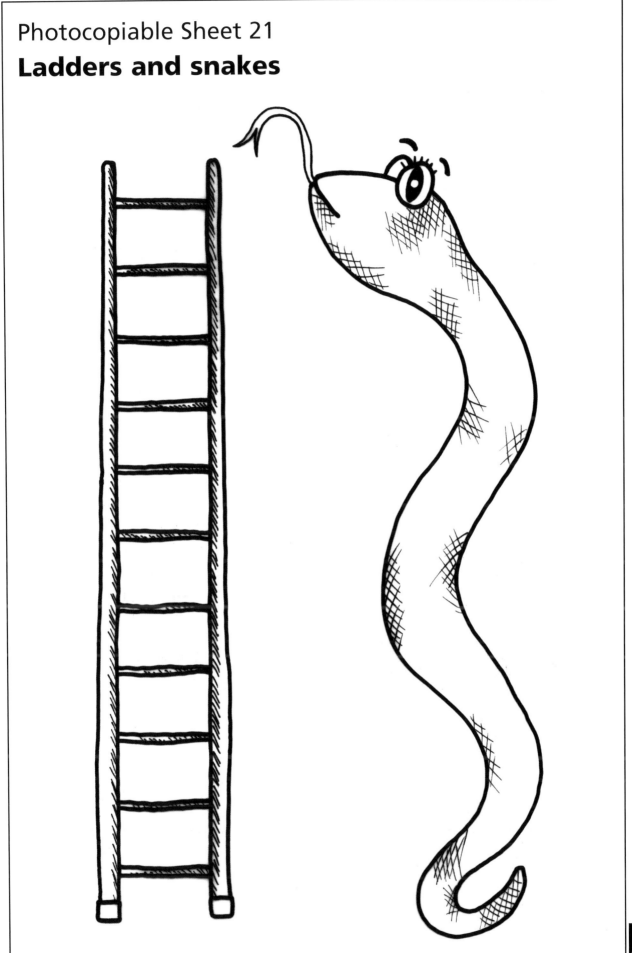

## Photocopiable Sheet 22
# Domino number game A

| | | | |
|---|---|---|---|
| **45** | **2 + 1** | **3** | **6 + 4** |
| **10** | **7 + 8** | **15** | **5 + 3** |
| **8** | **9 + 9** | **18** | **3 + 4** |
| **7** | **4 + 2** | **6** | **15 + 4** |
| **19** | **8 + 6** | **14** | **16 + 9** |
| **25** | **8 + 8** | **16** | **9 + 8** |
| **17** | **7 + 4** | **11** | **8 + 4** |
| **12** | **9 + 4** | **13** | **4 + 16** |

## Photocopiable Sheet 23

# Domino number game B

| 20 | 14 + 9 |
|---|---|

| 23 | 15 + 6 |
|---|---|

| 21 | 25 + 7 |
|---|---|

| 32 | 15 + 7 |
|---|---|

| 22 | 2 + 7 |
|---|---|

| 9 | 8 + 16 |
|---|---|

| 24 | 19 + 7 |
|---|---|

| 26 | 12 + 19 |
|---|---|

| 31 | 20 + 15 |
|---|---|

| 35 | 25 + 15 |
|---|---|

| 40 | 25 + 25 |
|---|---|

| 50 | 21 + 27 |
|---|---|

| 48 | 18 + 18 |
|---|---|

| 36 | 20 + 25 |
|---|---|

# Chapter 5
# Other ideas for an effective plenary

## Analysing the lesson

Discuss the lesson with the children to find out what they found the easiest/hardest/most enjoyable part of the lesson.
1. Ask the children what they found easy about the lesson and try to establish why they found this aspect easy. Focus on this during one plenary, and during other plenaries focus on the hardest and most enjoyable parts.
   Record their comments on the 'easy' parts as if brainstorming, for example:

*Year 2 brainstorm*

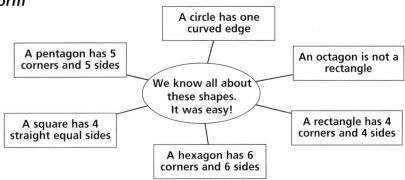

2. Have a vote to find out which was the most enjoyable part of the lesson and why. Use that information to build a bar chart with the class:

Children's comments:    'I enjoyed answering the problems.'  So did 5 others.
                        'I enjoyed the mental and oral starter.'  So did 7 others.
                        'I enjoyed making up my own problems.'  So did 4 others.
                        'I enjoyed working with my partner.'  So did 10 others.

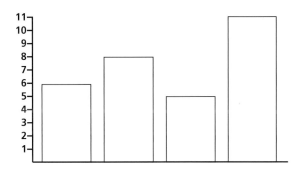

Invite some children to come to the board to construct it and add the labels.

3. Make a display of one of their favourite parts of the lesson, this can be used later as a prompt when the subject next comes up for example: make some statements on card or paper and invite a few children to match them with appropriate pictures:

---

## Year 1 display

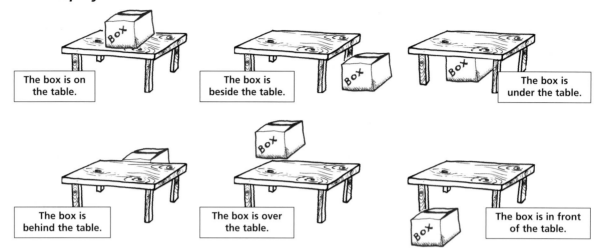

The box is on the table.

The box is beside the table.

The box is under the table.

The box is behind the table.

The box is over the table.

The box is in front of the table.

4. Discuss the most difficult part of the lesson and try to find out what made it so. Establish whether the children have a particular problem. Do not try to sort out any problems within this plenary as it may well take more time than is available, but make notes so that you can work on them again the next day or whenever is most appropriate.
Make a poster to show who has a difficulty and with what, but only do this if there is a large group of children with the same feeling. Remember to follow this up with another poster when they have succeeded:

## Year 1 poster

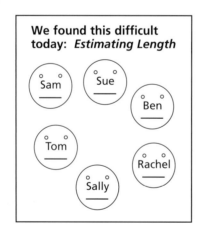

We found this difficult today: *Estimating Length*

Sam  Sue  Ben  Tom  Rachel  Sally

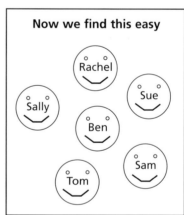

Now we find this easy

Rachel  Sally  Sue  Ben  Tom  Sam

# Identifying misconceptions

The above ideas help to identify any misconceptions that have occurred. If these are minor ones that can easily be sorted out, deal with them during the plenary, for example that this is a pentagon:

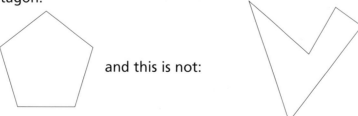

and this is not:

But of course, they both are.

If the misconceptions are more complicated, make a note of them and deal with them during the next numeracy session.

However, if you notice during individual, paired or group work that most children in the class are struggling with a common problem or misconception, then stop the lesson and go straight into a 'plenary' for the rest of the session in order to sort it out.

# Making general rules

Help the children to generalise a rule from examples generated by different groups. Examples of this might be:

1. Any number that ends in 9 can be added to another number by rounding it to the nearest 10 and subtracting one.
2. Dividing any number by four can be done by halving and halving again.
3. All six-sided shapes are hexagons.
4. Multiplying two numbers can be done in any order.
5. The sum of two odd numbers is always an even number.
6. You can check subtraction sums by adding the answer to one of the other numbers. If your answer is correct you will always get the third number.

# Reflection

You can use the plenary to draw together what has been learned, reflect on what was important in the lesson, summarise key facts, ideas and vocabulary and what needs to be remembered.

This needs to be discussion based. There should be lots of interaction with the children. Ask them appropriate questions, listen to them talking about their work and discuss what they think is the important aspect to remember.

Make sure that you summarise key facts, ideas and objectives for the children and review the vocabulary that they should have learnt.

# Drawing it together

At the end of a unit of work, draw together what has been learnt over a series of lessons. This again needs to be a discussion-based session. There should be lots of interaction with the children. Ask them appropriate questions and listen to them talking about their work. At the end of a unit it is important to draw together what has been learnt over the series of lessons by summarising key facts, ideas and objectives.

# Consolidating and developing

During the plenary session, recap what has been learnt briefly and then develop the work a stage further, for example:

1. After a Year 2 lesson investigating numbers on a number square, review and then go on to look at the square, pretending that it goes from 100 – 200.
2. Following a very practical Year 1 lesson on counting objects, use the plenary session to develop the work by discussing ways in which the number of objects can be recorded.

# Celebrate success in the children's work

Discuss with the children whether they think they have been successful during their group or whole-class work. Remind them of the objective of the lesson: do they think they have achieved it? Ask for comments. Ask them to give an example of the work they have completed. Then try one of the following:

1. Invite other children to say something positive to the child, pair or group about their particular success.
2. Give the child/pair/group a clap.
3. Have a success poster or sheet on the wall and write that success and the children's names beside it, for example:

## This week we are learning about odd and even numbers

Peter, Bobby, Sam and Jenny know that multiples of 10 are always even numbers.

Katie now knows that an odd number ends with 1, 3, 5, 7 or 9.

Add to this over the week and continue with it next time the topic is revisited, so that every child will see his/her name on the chart over a period of time. Add any small success: this is particularly important for those children who lack confidence.

Award points or merits for success. You could display them on a poster, for example:

## We have succeeded!

Ben

Adam

Maggie

At the end of a topic, if the children have worked well and achieved success, have a celebration party, playing lots of maths games and having a drink and biscuit. Create a special plenary by inviting other children or the head of the school along to share these successes with them.

# Number cards A

| | | | |
|---|---|---|---|
| 0 | 1 | 2 | 3 |
| 4 | 5 | 6 | 7 |
| 8 | 9 | 10 | 11 |
| 12 | 13 | 14 | 15 |
| 16 | 17 | 18 | 19 |
| 20 | 21 | 22 | 23 |

# Number cards B

| | | | |
|---|---|---|---|
| **24** | **25** | **26** | **27** |
| **28** | **29** | **30** | **31** |
| **32** | **33** | **34** | **35** |
| **36** | **37** | **38** | **39** |
| **40** | **41** | **42** | **43** |
| **44** | **45** | | |